AF432025

Credits

Native American Cultures: Myths and magic / Mendoza Vester, Jorge

© 2023 Native American Cultures: Myths and magic - Jorge Mendoza Vester

1st edition.- City of Santiago, Chile , 2023

www.historiayleyendas.com

First edition digital book

NATIVE AMERICAN CULTURES

Myths and magic

CONTENTS

HISTORY...11
Native Americans: Challenging Stereotypes 11
The Importance of Knowledge of Native Cultures.............................12
The Contribution of the Book to Understanding Native Cultures.....12
North America: A Legacy of Ancient Cultures 12
The Origins of Native Americans in North America...........................13
The Native Oral Tradition: A Fabric of Tales.............................15
The Native Population of North America Before European Arrival .16
The Settlement of North America 17

POPULATION AND TERRITORIES 21
The Peoples of the Northeast 21
Forests and Southeast...26
The Great Basin 29
Northwestern..30
The Great Plains 32
Southwest..35
California 37
Chaco Canyon 38
The northwest coast and plateau 39
Sub-Arctic..42

CULTURES, CUSTOMS, WORLDVIEW...45
Sacred History 45
Creation Stories 48
Myths of Creation 50
Mythology of the Navajo 54
North America. The Iroquois tribes 58
The Origins of Humanity..58
Animals..60
The Sacred Pipe 65
Ritual dances...67
Social organization..71
Medicinal plants..85

SPIRITUAL LIFE...89
Animism..89
Shamans and healers 90
The Beyond 90
The quest for vision 92

The Shaman's Call...96
The relationship between humans and animals.......................96
The world is renewing. 97
The Preservation of the Sacred..98
The Ceremonial Transformations 103
Food for body and soul: cactus 104
Shamans...105
The world of the four worlds. 105
The gods yei...106
Sacred team games..107
Humanity's Relatives 107
Divine Beings...108
Dreams...113
Nature and spirit 114
Supernatural Beings..115

TRADITIONS, MYTHS, STORIES AND LEGENDS 119
Narrations 119
The legend of the okanagan and shuswap tribes in Canada............119
What's the reason behind the porcupine quills ornament?.............120
Mocking and mischievous...120
Salmon and coyote..121
The crown symbolizes light..122
The Coyote Route..123
The heart of the brave antelope 123
The bear 124
The thunderbird...125
Windigo 126
Scammers combine entertainment and wickedness. 126
The painful lesson of the great Hare 127
The liberation of wild animals 127
The sun woman, the spider grandmother and the twins.............129
The stone can tell stories. 130
The Sacred Clowns 131
Animal Myths..131
Nanabozho 132
Little Star 133
Why is the polar star still? 134
Totemic posts 135
The almizclerous mouse, diving in the ground.....................135
Spider rock, house of the spider woman 136

HEROES, RELEVANT PEOPLE..................................139

Divinities and Heroes...139
Heroes...140
Cultural Heroes...140
Louise Erdrich...143
Black Alce..143
Big Thunder talks about the earth...144
The Chief Joseph..144
The Prophet Shawnee..145
Glooskap and Malsum..146
Iroquois...146
The main figures...148
Literature..154
Nativist Movements..155

TERRITORIAL CONFLICTS **159**
Current territorial conflicts...159
Crow Creek...161
Wounded Knee...161
The great mound of the serpent..163
The Bear's Hill (Bear Butte)..165
The train...166
Schools for Indians..166
Until the seventh generation..168
Languages...169
The Battle of Little Bighorn...170
The Native American Church...172
The Impact of Christianity...173
Modern Medicine...174
Loss of land..174
The opposite side of the story...176
Reserves..177
Forced displacement..178
Encrypted speakers..180
Live past..180
Historical Claims..181
The return of Ahayuda...182

HAU DE NO SAU NEE "PEOPLE WHO BUILD" **185**
Message to the Western World...185

HISTORY

Native Americans: Challenging Stereotypes

Native North Americans, an integral part of the world's most culturally diverse population, have historically been misunderstood and labeled in contradictory ways. In the 18th century, they were called "noble savages," and today some recognize them as "the first environmentalists." In cinema, we have seen them portrayed in various ways, from bloodthirsty savages to pacifist victims of "progress."

These contradictory representations highlight the ambivalence of attitudes towards indigenous people. On one hand, they are perceived as primitive and traditional in contrast to modern and complex white society. On the other hand, they are considered wise, respectful of the land, and advocates of a lifestyle that honors the planet.

Native peoples react in different ways to these perceptions. They reject images that depict them as barbaric and are wary of those who take their beliefs out of context. However, some indigenous individuals do not mind if some non-natives interpret their cultures as models of environmental conservation.

Respect is a fundamental value for indigenous people. Those who do not share their beliefs should not interfere with what they consider sacred or appropriate their traditions in pursuit of their own spiritual redemption. It is important to recognize that indigenous peoples have valid ways of understanding the world that differ from Western science and history.

Indigenous people have the right to reject archaeological theories that deny their millennia-old oral traditions, as these are essential to their identity. Non-natives must understand that their knowledge of indigenous people is limited, and they cannot assume that they know what it means to be indigenous.

Indigenous people are not simply relics of the past; they remain a living part of the modern world, with rich, flexible, and adaptable cultures that have survived the challenges of the centuries since the arrival of Europeans in North America. By maintaining their ancestral traditions, they have demonstrated a remarkable ability to adapt to modern changes and challenges. Their struggle to preserve their identity and their relationship with the land is a testament to their resilience.

This diverse group of indigenous peoples not only deserves respect for their unique cultural heritage but also a deeper understanding of their ongoing role in today's society. Beyond stereotypes and changing perceptions, Native Americans are an essential part of North America's rich tapestry of history, with a present and a future that deserve to be understood and respected.

The Importance of Knowledge of Native Cultures

To break the deeply rooted stereotypes in society about Native Americans, it is essential to delve into the richness and complexity of their cultures. These cultures have unique histories, traditions, and perspectives that have often been misunderstood or overlooked. Gaining in-depth knowledge of their way of life, spiritual beliefs, social systems, and their relationship with the land is a fundamental step in eliminating biases and appreciating the diversity that enriches North America.

The Contribution of the Book to Understanding Native Cultures

This book serves as a window into the understanding of Native American cultures. Through the exploration of their myths and legends, the roots of their worldview and core values are unveiled. The stories contained within these pages provide a unique opportunity to delve into the heart of these cultures, revealing deep connections with nature, spirituality, and community.

This book not only challenges deep-seated stereotypes but also offers an enriching perspective that contributes to a more comprehensive and respectful appreciation of the indigenous peoples of North America. By understanding their histories, myths, and traditions, we are taking an important step toward cultural reconciliation and the appreciation of the diversity that has enriched the history of this land.

North America: A Legacy of Ancient Cultures

Since the arrival of their ancestors in North America, between 12,000 and 60,000 years ago, the indigenous peoples of this continent have forged a rich diversity of cultures, many of which have been passed down through generations via oral traditions. These traditions endure in the reservations where some of the Native Americans reside today. Historically, the structure of these societies has varied considerably, largely influenced by the environment in which they settled, whether as nomadic hunters or sedentary farmers.

For Native Americans, religion permeates every aspect of life and their relationship with nature. Myths play a sacred role in their beliefs, as they help explain the cosmic and social order, as well as the interactions between gods and humans. Among these myths, the most relevant ones narrate the actions of deities, especially those related to the creation and fundamental structure of the universe, the origins of humanity, death, the significance of corn, and animal hunting. Often, the narration of these myths is restricted to specific moments or seasons, adding a ceremonial component to their transmission.

"Institutional" myths also play a significant role, recounting how culture and human institutions emerged, often thanks to the intervention of a primordial cultural hero who provided the first guidelines to human ancestors. These "ritual" myths form the basis of sacred ceremonies, in which the stories are ritually reenacted under specific circumstances, as seen in the Hopi ceremonies, where segments of the "emergence" myth are performed. These myths take center stage in agrarian societies.

On the other hand, "entertainment" myths, narrated with the purpose of entertaining and conveying moral teachings, allow for a greater freedom of interpretation. Many of these myths involve clever and playful characters who often impart important lessons.

We will delve deep into these rich mythological and cultural traditions, providing a more comprehensive and respectful insight into the indigenous peoples of North America. Through an understanding of their myths and beliefs, we hope to contribute to dispelling deep-seated stereotypes and fostering greater respect for the cultural diversity that has enriched this continent over millennia.

The Origins of Native Americans in North America

The history of Native Americans in North America dates back an astonishing 60,000 years. In this distant past, a significant number of people began to migrate from the vast, warm plains of central Asia to the region of Siberia in the northeast. However, their journey didn't stop there; they crossed the Chukotka Peninsula to reach America, taking advantage of a land or ice bridge that connected Chukotka to what is now Alaska.

These ancient inhabitants were hunters and gatherers, living in harmony with the herds of game that roamed the lands. From their initial settlements in Alaska, many generations traveled down the Columbia River to the warmer southern regions. In their journey, they crossed the imposing Rocky Mountains and encountered a diversity of peoples, some strange, with whom they had various interactions. There were often conflicts, but they also joined some of these communities.

Throughout the ages, Native Americans continued their migration, following the routes of bison and buffalo, moving eastward to the Atlantic coast, and southward to the regions of the Sierra Madre Oriental, the Mexican plains, rainforests, and jungles of the Yucatán. As they settled in new territories, they developed a rich variety of skills and crafts, including mastery of the bow and arrow, flint toolmaking, basket weaving, and clay pottery.

These migrations reached so far that today, one can still find slight similarities in language, culture, and physical appearance between the indigenous peoples of Peru and Bolivia and the Inuit of Siberia and Alaska. Similarly, connections can be observed between the Huron and Iroquois in New York state with the Chukchi and Koryak of northeastern Siberia.

As these tribes explored and settled vast expanses of land, they multiplied like the sand in the sea, giving rise to an impressive linguistic diversity, with at least around 3,000 distinct languages in use. However, they were constantly under pressure to adapt and move due to changing conditions and needs.

A critical point in their history arrived in 1492 with the arrival of Christopher Columbus in the New World. Although he believed he had reached the shores of India, Columbus mistakenly called them "Indians." The English continued the error with their term "Indians," and the French used the term "peaux rouges," meaning redskins.

Over the four centuries that followed, from 1492 to 1890, Native Americans witnessed the invasion and colonization of their lands. During that time, much of their cultures and civilizations were profoundly affected and, in many cases, destroyed. However, their legacy endures as an essential part of the rich history of North America.

The Native Oral Tradition: A Fabric of Tales

The oral tradition of Native Americans is a rich and complex source of narratives in which it is often difficult to distinguish between myths and other forms of storytelling. In their language, people commonly use terms like "stories," which can range from "true stories" recounting events from the present world to "mythical stories" describing events that occurred in ancient times, long before the appearance of humans.

Since these cultures lack a writing system, these stories were not recorded on paper until colonizers began documenting them in the 1830s. In ancient times, in every community, there was at least one wise elder who held the knowledge of these narratives. It was their task to represent these stories in a memorable manner, often embodying various characters through grunts, shouts, roars, or moans, making the stories come to life.

Before the U.S. government confined native tribes to reservations, different indigenous communities had intense contact with each other, resulting in an enriching exchange of stories. This led to the spread of the same stories, though with variations and nuances, that could be found across the continent. This phenomenon underscores the deep connection between Native peoples and the significance of their narratives in the history of North America.

Out of the approximately 300 languages that thrived in North America before the arrival of Europeans, about 200 of them have been preserved. These languages are spoken by roughly three-quarters of a million people. The linguistic diversity is astonishing, ranging from languages with a considerable number of speakers, like Navajo, which has 160,000 speakers, to critically endangered languages, like Chinook, spoken by only 30 individuals.

Below is a chronological table outlining key milestones in the history of Native Americans in North America:

- 60,000-12,000 years ago: The first peoples arrive in North America from northeastern Asia, crossing land or ice, marking the beginning of a rich history.

- 10,000-8,000 years ago: The first cultures emerge, laying the foundations for the complex societies that will develop on the continent.

- 1000-1300 AD: The expansion of Athabascan languages, such as Apache and Navajo, is due to migrations from Canada to the southwest.

- 1600-1750 AD: Peoples like the Cheyenne and Dakota settle on the vast plains of North America. The arrival of horses, introduced by the Spanish, revolutionizes warfare and hunting in the region.

- 1830-1840 AD: The United States forcibly removes most natives living east of the Mississippi River to the west, marking a period of forced displacement.

- 1890: The U.S. cavalry carries out the massacre of 200 Dakota in Wounded Knee, South Dakota, ending Native resistance against white population expansion.

The Native Population of North America Before European Arrival

The estimation of the indigenous population in North America before the arrival of Europeans has been a subject of debate among scholars. Since there is no definitive record, several attempts have been made to calculate this figure based on various factors. In the early years of the last century, James Mooney of the Smithsonian Institution estimated the population of each tribe before contact, arriving at a figure slightly over one million, which clearly appears to be conservative.

In the late 1960s, Henry Dobyns, using depopulation rates, obtained estimates ranging from 9.8 to 12.2 million inhabitants. In 1983, he repeated his calculations, taking into account the environment's capacity to support the population, and arrived at a total figure of 18 million inhabitants. Other scholars, such as Douglas Ubelaker and Russell Thornton, also employed depopulation rates but obtained figures close to 1,800,000 inhabitants.

Today, Thornton proposes an estimate that hovers around seven million. It is possible that future analyses will yield a clearer consensus, but so far, most experts agree that the native population of North America immediately before the arrival of Europeans did not exceed ten million.

What is widely accepted by specialists is the devastating population decline of Native Americans due to diseases introduced to America by the early Europeans and Africans. Epidemic diseases wreaked havoc among the indigenous populations, which had no prior exposure to these diseases and, therefore, lacked immunity. The most deadly diseases included smallpox, influenza, and measles, which decimated entire communities. Between 1781 and 1856, four smallpox and whooping cough outbreaks reduced the population of tribes like the Arikara, Mandan, and Hidatsa, all of whom were farmers living in villages along the Missouri River in Dakota, from over 35,000 to less than 2,000 inhabitants. Diseases like typhus, scarlet fever, diphtheria, mumps, and cholera also took a heavy toll on indigenous populations.

Disease played a crucial role in the drastic decline of the indigenous population, although factors such as war, deliberate genocide, which included forced displacement, relocations, and famine, also contributed. Not all diseases were introduced accidentally: in 1763, the British military commander of Pennsylvania ordered the intentional delivery of smallpox-infected blankets to indigenous communities. Furthermore, until the late 20th century, some Indian Health Service doctors are reported to have sterilized indigenous women without their consent. The disappearance of traditional healing practices due to the destruction of ancestral ways of life also contributed to the decline.

Around 1900, the indigenous population had decreased to less than one million, making the recovery they experienced in the 20th century remarkable. This recovery was due in part to improvements in healthcare and the increase in fertility resulting from interracial marriages.

According to the 1990 U.S. census, the combined population of Native Americans, Eskimos (Inuit), and Aleuts approached two million. When adding the 740,000 Canadian natives, which include Indigenous, Inuit, and Métis, the total population of Native Americans in North America in 2000 approaches three million.

However, determining precise figures is complicated due to the difficulty of defining who is considered indigenous and who is not. The number of people self-identifying as indigenous has significantly increased. According to some estimates, nearly seven million Americans have indigenous ancestry, and the growing interest in native culture leads more people to recognize their roots. The Bureau of Indian Affairs uses a "blood quantum" system, which requires at least one indigenous grandparent to be considered "indigenous." However, tribes have their own criteria; some require at least "half-indigenous," while others accept an indigenous great-great-grandparent, and a few only require documentary evidence of indigenous ancestry.

The Settlement of North America

The settlement of North America took place during the last glacial period known as the "Wisconsinan glaciation." During this era, glacial advances lowered sea levels due to ice accumulation, resulting in the exposure of a land bridge in the Bering Strait connecting Siberia and Alaska. It is assumed that through this land bridge, known as Beringia, humans moved from Northeast Asia to North America, from where they gradually dispersed across the continent. The migration routes, which still generate debates, illustrate how humans moved inland through ice-free corridors during brief periods of thaw.

Traces of the early inhabitants of North America are often buried under layers of sediment accumulated over thousands of years. Direct evidence of early human presence, whether in the form of stone tools, animal remains, fire sites, or structures, is rarely discovered unless they emerge due to valley slope erosion or are accidentally unearthed under debris from shelters or stone caves. However, every find, no matter how modest, contributes to the reconstruction of human life in North America during the last glacial period.

Available archaeological materials indicate that over ten thousand years ago, groups of hunter-gatherers lived in geographically distant regions. These areas included the Northeast, the Western Plains, the Southwest, and northern Alaska. In this ancient world, the population was sparse, and these groups hunted a variety of animals, including mammoths, mastodons, giant bison, and medium and small-sized animals like deer and rabbits. Hunters moved according to the availability of game and lived in temporary shelters, reflecting a nomadic lifestyle that persisted in the subarctic forests of northern Canada until relatively recent times.

The Oldest Human Findings in America date from a much later time compared to those found in Asia. During the last ice age, the Beringia land bridge connected North America and Asia into one continent. This geography, along with the physical similarities between Native peoples of North America and those from northern Asia, suggests the possibility of mammoth hunters coming to America from the west. Over the past 40,000 years, although extensive glaciers covered much of the north, there were periods of warmer climates that created ice-free corridors extending into the interior of the continent. One of these corridors likely followed the coast, while others were located parallel to the eastern edge of the Rocky Mountains.

However, the opportunity to migrate across Beringia came to an end due to climate warming, the last ice retreat, and rising sea levels, which led to the submersion of the land bridge. The theory that human occupation of the continent is relatively recent is based on the lack of archaeological sites in North America that can be securely dated before 15,000 BCE. However, evidence found in South America suggests a much more complex pattern of occupation. In the southern region, such as in Patagonia, sites have been found dating as early as in North America. This suggests that humans may have migrated to North America much earlier than initially thought.

Recent excavations in Brazil have yielded surprising findings, including artifacts that archaeologists estimate could be over 30,000 years old. These discoveries indicate the possibility that humans moved to North America at a time when Beringia did not yet exist as a land bridge. While the absence of irrefutable evidence of human presence in North America before approximately 15,000 BCE remains a mystery, this complex and ever-evolving scenario reveals a fascinating history of migration and settlement on the continent.

The discussion about the settlement of North America goes beyond the existence or absence of dated evidence. Europeans, with their inclination toward scientific solutions, often focus on migratory hypotheses derived from the analysis of archaeological sites, artifacts, chronological sequences, and maps. However, a fundamental fact is often overlooked: the early inhabitants of North America did not see themselves as emigrants leaving one continent to start a new life on another. Instead, they lived their daily lives and moved in search of game animals.

Another perspective to understand human presence in America suggests that people have occupied this land since time immemorial. This idea is rooted in the traditions of many indigenous cultures and still persists as a significant religious and political issue today. The mythologies of various contemporary indigenous groups, such as the Ojibwa and Hopi, tell stories of the first people who wandered from the place of origin to their later homes. Creation stories also reflect the way of life of each group. For example, creation narratives in agricultural communities refer to the emergence of the land in specific places in the landscape. Meanwhile, stories of traditional hunter-gatherer groups reflect their lives dedicated to hunting animals or visionary quests.

As the climate became warmer and drier, glaciers and tundra retreated northward, giving way to meadows and forests. Large animals from the glacial period disappeared, possibly hunted to extinction. Humans adapted their lives to focus on hunting and gathering. Over time, advances like the bow, arrow, and pottery developed. In regions with favorable climate and fertile soil, people began to cultivate maize, beans, and other crops. The introduction of agriculture allowed for the rise of great civilizations in fertile valleys like the Mississippi and Ohio rivers, where cities, earthworks, impressive artwork, and complex religious belief systems were built. In other areas, populations continued their hunting, fishing, and gathering traditions.

The inhabitants of North America did not remain static or isolated in the millennia leading up to the arrival of the Europeans. They traveled great distances to exchange materials, such as stones and shells, which they used to create tools and ornaments, respectively. As these groups moved from one place to another, different languages emerged and spread. The extent of this activity is evident in the fact that today, people who speak related languages are separated by vast distances. The languages of the Navajo and Apache in the southwest have connections to those of hunters in Alaska and the Yukon Territory.

Therefore, just before the European invasion, North America was a place where humans had thrived for at least fifteen millennia, and possibly much longer. The drastic changes that were triggered and had a devastating impact on indigenous populations were largely due to profound differences in understanding that separated native cultures from European ones. From the perspective of Native Americans, the land was a place occupied, managed, and known, while white explorers and colonizers only saw an empty expanse waiting to be conquered.

POPULATION AND TERRITORIES

The Peoples of the Northeast

The northeastern region of North America is characterized by its abundance of forests, lakes and rivers. It extends from the cold, steep land eroded by glaciers north of the Great Lakes and the San Lorenzo River, to the extensive, warm coastal plains of the Atlantic, including the Mississippi and Ohio valleys.

In the northern regions of this cultural area, where the enormous pine trees and picea forests of the sub-Arctic dominated the landscape, residents faced late frostbite and early freezes that jeopardized crops, such as corn, cultivated by their southern neighbours. Tribes such as the Ojibwas, Abenakis, Micmac, and other northern Algonquin groups led a nomadic life. They sailed in canoes of beetle bark through lakes and extensive waterway systems, following stations for hunting, harvesting and fishing.

The ancient ancestors of the southern tribes, who engaged in horticulture, probably shared a similar lifestyle. Highly mobile hunter camps have been discovered dating back to as early as 16,000 BC, a time when glaciations still covered the north.

In their travels, Algonquin speakers often built simple tipis or conical stores made of tree bark or animal skins. For summer and winter camps, which were more permanent and from where they went out to collect food, complex conical structures were erected of stacks covered with beech or straw bark, or animal skins, known as wigwams.

These communities in the northern forests depended on a wide range of vegetable foods, ranging from wild rice and lake grasses to strawberries. They also competed with bears for this food that grew on the slopes of the hills after the forest fires. The hunt was centered on animals such as deer and deer, who were seen as gifts of animal spirits and, at times, considered ancestors of hunters. The micmac, for example, erected stone prey, used branch fishing techniques to catch angels, and used open sea canoes to hunt marsopes.

Lifestyle and Cultural Development in the South of the Great Lakes

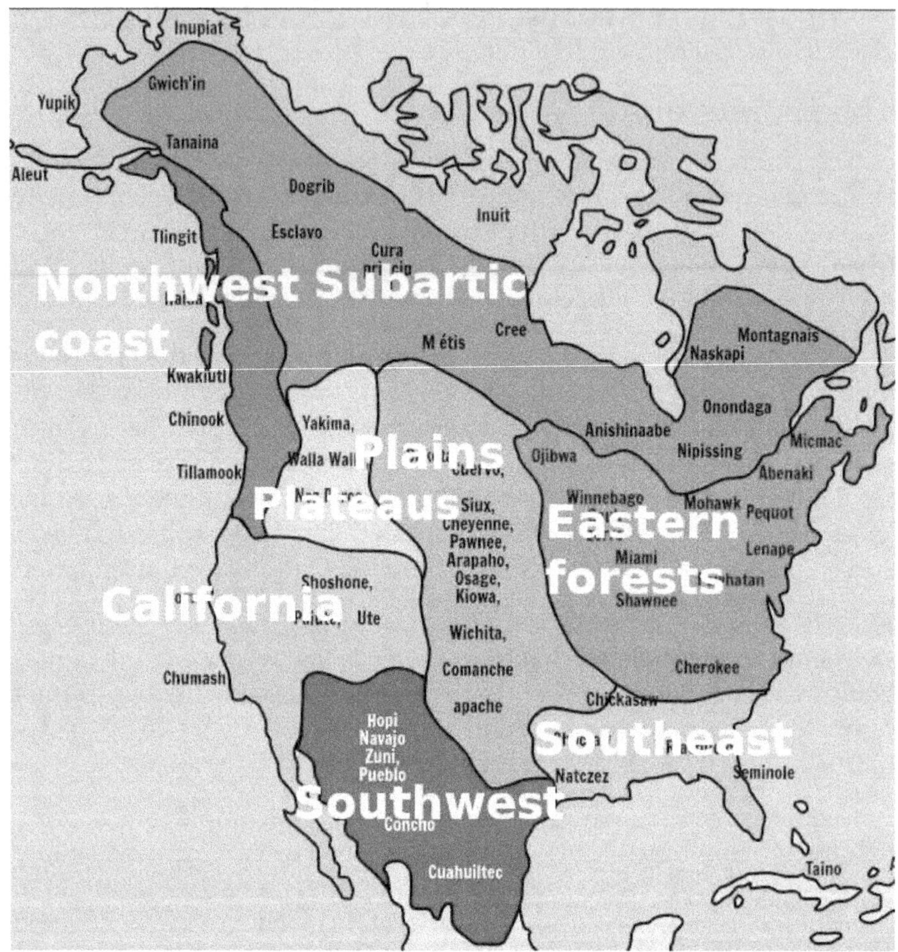

The need for seminomed life decreased south of the Superior and Erie lakes, where rich soils covered the solid rock, and the sturdy abets and piceas were replaced by pine trees and leafy trees. With longer summers and less severe winters, it became possible to grow maize, eggs and shrimp. Algonquin tribes such as the Illinois, Southern Ojibwas and Menominis developed a more stable way of life compared to their northern neighbours. This also applied to the winnebagos and other Sioux-speaking groups, as well as the delawars, wampanoags and other natives of the Atlantic coast.

Although hunting and harvesting remained important, especially for those engaged in the harvest of seafood and other marine resources, agriculture became the pillar of their lives. The importance of agriculture is evident in the mound-building crops that developed in the fertile river valleys around 500 B.C.E. The culture of Adena, who were initially hunters and gatherers, flourished in the Ohio valley thanks to the abundance of resources, allowing them to carry out complex rituals and ceremonies that were embodied in imposing mounds, such as the Great Serpent Hill.

A few centuries later, with the emergence of Hopewell culture in the same region, society became even more hierarchical and sophisticated. Unlike surrounding societies that were relatively egalitarian, Hopewell's culture focused its creativity on the social and religious elite. His legacy includes masterpieces in stone, ceramics, wood and metal, as well as a monumental complex of ceremonial mounds near the present-day city of Hopewell, Ohio, which gave the name to this culture. For about half a millennium, the inhabitants of Hopewell influenced the cultural life of the Middle West, from the Great Lakes to the Gulf of Mexico.

The Skin Exchange

In 1615, during his cohabitation with the Hurons, Samuel de Champlain observed that the women of the tribe grinded corn and exchanged it with their Algonquin neighbors in exchange for leather and other forest resources. Champlain and other European merchants also had an interest in leather, but their demand went beyond the small trade between tribes. They offered guns, knives, stoves, fabrics, alcoholic beverages and other commercial products in exchange for leather. The introduction of some of these European items had a negative impact on indigenous culture, as it emphasized hunting and displaced traditional manufacturing. Alcohol, in particular, had devastating effects on tribal life.

By 1635, the castor population had virtually exhausted in the territory of the Hurons, which led these tribes to obtain skins through trade with the nipissing and ottawas. However, the Iroquois also engaged in the leather trade and competed with the Hurons when their resources were exhausted. In 1649, the Iroquois attacked the Hurons and took control of the leather trade in the region.

By the mid-19th century, castor leather hats ceased to be a fashion in Europe, causing a drastic decline in demand for this product. In addition, in the forests of northeastern North America, the castor population decreased considerably.

The Lacrosse Game

Lacrosse is a sport practiced by many groups of North American Indians, known for its violent character and the physical contact between the two teams that are located at the ends of a large field. The name "lacrosse" comes from the French word "la crosse", which means "the rod." This name was coined by a 17th-century French missionary, who compared the curved sticks used by the players with the bishop's bow.

The game involves moving a wooden ball with a stick that has a net at the end, and the goal is to make the ball cross the poles of the goal of the opposing team, passing it between players as many times as necessary to it. During the first period of European occupation in the region, lacrosse matches used to take place between villages, and teams often consisted of up to a hundred players, with hundreds of spectators. It is important to note that lacrosse was more than just a game; the Iroquois, who are attributed to the modern form of Lacrosse, regarded it as a gift from the Creator and practised it ceremonially in events such as seeding and harvest rituals, as a way to honor spirits.

The Petroglyphs of Peterborough

In the vicinity of Lake Stony, in Peterborough County, Ontario, Canada, there is a fascinating archaeological site where ancient artists carved hundreds of images onto an outstanding white, crystal clear limestone wall. Per the unique appearance of the rock attracted these prehistoric artists. Over time, erosion has created a series of holes, cracks, and oaknesses that seem to sink into the depths of the underground world. During the spring, these characteristics become even more noticeable due to the dampened sounds of groundwater emanating from the ground. It is plausible that those who created these images would consider this place to be magical or hear the voices of spirits in these sounds.

Archaeological excavations in the ground and the remains found in some cracks have revealed fragments of ceramics and various stone tools. These artifacts suggest that the carpenters worked in this place for a period ranging from half a century to a millennium.

The site of Peterborough is exceptional due to the diversity of the images it contains. These range from figures of animals and birds to human representations, evoking similarities to the cave paintings and petroglyphs from other sites in the region. In addition, some of the images include large solar boats that surprisingly resemble Scandinavian sizes.

The Ojibwas refer to th[em] "the rock that teaches." For indigenous peoples, Peterborough is a place of spiritual reflection and inspiration.

Today, these cave paintings are part of the Petroglyphs Provincial Park and are protected from erosion by an aluminum and glass building. The Ojibwa community is responsible for the maintenance and management of this archaeological site.

Using stone tools, Peterborough artists recorded more than nine hundred figures, including animals, humans, turtles, snakes, canoes and other images on the smooth, crystal clear li-

mestone surface of the rock. However, centuries of freezing and unfreezing cycles have increased the erosion of the crystal surface, making the originally clear, well-defined images hardly visible today. To allow modern generations to appreciate its beauty and variety, archaeologists J. M. and R. K. Vastokas darkened the petroglyphs. Although the artists who created them remain anonymous, they are likely to have been ancestors of the Algonquin peoples, such as the Ojibwas, who still reside in the region. These cave paintings are a testimony to the rich artistic tradition of the Algonquins, as evidenced by the paintings extending through the vast rocky region known as the "Canadian Shield" and the sacred art engraved in beetle bark rolls by the Midéwewins.

One of the most notable representations in Peterborough is a boat that stands out from all traditional Aboriginal boats. The proa and the popa are elongated and curved upwards, while the mast bears the solar symbol. Similar ships that include celestial images are only found in Scandinavia.

Forests and Southeast

Much of North and East America is characterized by its extensive coverage of dense forests, interrupted only by the presence of lakes and rivers. The myths that flourished in this region, with their stories about spirits, demons and forest monsters, faithfully reflect the natural environment. Here, elemental gods were worshipped and one believed in a supreme being, in addition to conceiving a higher and a lower world. Despite pressure from European settlers, some of the native inhabitants migrated to the plains, but managed to preserve much of their rich mythology.

Southeast

From the wavy Apalachian mountains to the region that encompasses Florida and the coast of the Gulf of Mexico, and to the west, from beyond the Lower Mississippi to the arid lowlands of southeastern Texas, extends a warm, humid and fertile region. In this environment, the diversity of vegetation and animal life was exceptional. Most of the inhabitants of this region were farmers who lived in villages. Unlike their northern counterparts, these southern farmers harvested maize twice a year, in addition to growing shrimp and sunflower. In the subtropical areas near the Gulf of Mexico, bananas, rice, bonia and sugarcane were also grown.

Peoples, such as the Florida caluses, continued to be hunting and harvesting, taking advantage of the abundance of birds, reptiles, fish, whales and foxes, as well as the edible roots of the subtropical Atlantic coastline and the Gulf of Mexico. The forests and open spaces of the interior offered a rich source of edible fruit, wild dried fruit and hunting animals, while the rivers were full of fish.

Hunting in this region required special techniques, as there was no snow that slowed down the speeds of deer. Many of the hunters perfected the calls to attract the frogs and keep them away from their weapons.

Traditional housing varied by tribe, but the creeks, for example, built rectangular summer houses with two-water roofs and adobe walls, and winter houses in a conical form, partially buried to isolate from the cold. In subtropical areas, housing was designed to withstand warm climates, like seedlings houses, which were open structures with roofs of palm leaves.

The abundance and diversity of plants in the southeastern region suggests that the indigenous tribes of this area had extensive knowledge of the medicinal properties of herbs and used numerous plant substances in their ritual practices. They cultivated tobacco, smoked in pipes during ceremonies or applied it to their bodies for healing purposes.

In the late 15th century, when the Spaniards arrived in this region, the south-eastern tribes still retained attributes of the Mississippi culture, the last of the great cultures of the river valleys of North America. They spoke different languages: the Creeks, the Choctaw and the Chickasaw used dialects of the Muskogi, the Catawbas spoke Sioux and the Cherokis expressed themselves in Iroquois. The cultural complexity of the region was affected by the first contacts with Europeans, which began with the Spanish expedition of 1513. Successive Spanish, French, and English invasions, along with the arrival of American settlers, triggered wars, diseases, and disorder in indigenous communities, accelerating their decline.

However, the most devastating blow to the Southeast tribes came with President Andrew Jackson, who enacted the Indian Removal Act of 1830, which prohibited Aborigines from staying east of Mississippi. This measure mainly affected the "five civilized tribes" that had worked to assimilate to the white culture: the choctaw, the chickasaw, the seminolas, the creek and the cherokis. Most of these groups were displaced to the west, often through forced marches that resulted in the deaths of thousands of people. The Cherokee, for example, referred to their displacement as the "trail of tears," an expression adopted by other indigenous nations.

The cheroki syllable

Cherokee emerged as the first indigenous language to have a writing system, thanks to the syllable developed by Sequoyah (1770-1843). He devoted more than ten years of his life to creating this system, which succeeded in reducing the cherokee to eighty-six distinct syllables. The introduction of this syllable was received with remarkable enthusiasm, and in 1824 the Bible was published in Cherokee, marking an important milestone.

Four years later, two additional milestones appeared: The Cherokee Phoenix, a bilingual newspaper, and the Constitution written in cherokee. During the first half of the 19th century, this silabary played a fundamental role in preserving Cherokee culture from the pressure and oppression of white culture.

Cahokia

Cahokia, an ancient settlement in North America near the Mississippi River, about 11 km from the present St. Louis, Missouri, represented the main urban center before the 19th century. Its development began with a small agricultural village founded between the years 600 and 800. The inhabitants of this region planted corn in the fertile drainage plain, similar to what the Hopewell settlers had previously done. However, in Cahokia, hybrid varieties of corn were used, similar to those grown in Mexico, which were more resistant and produced abundant crops. Thanks to this wealth, Cahokia and other villages in the Mississippi River area and its tributaries progressed and grew.

These Mississippi settlements were characterized by the presence of large mounds and squares, which shared surprising similarities with Mesoamerican temple and square complexes. For example, in Moundville, Alabama, there were 20 mounds arranged in circles, some of them used as graves and others as temples and residences for the elite. Aztalán, a fortified city in Wisconsin, was located next to impressive mountains with sculptures of animals and birds, built by an earlier culture. However, Cahokia stood out as the most complex urban center that developed in northern Mexico.

When the Spaniards explored the Mississippi River in the 16th century, Cahokia had long been abandoned. Overpopulation, which led to epidemics, social conflicts and droughts, may have been one of the causes of the decline of Cahokia and the Mississippi cities in general.

At its peak, between 850 and 1150, Cahokia had more than a hundred pyramids and mounds of land with flat peaks, of which approximately twenty can still be seen today. Although in the past, large wooden structures were erected over these mounds, possibly used as residences for high-ranking people, the majority of the population lived in smaller wooden buildings, arranged around the mounds and squares. It is estimated that the population may have exceeded 10,000 inhabitants, with up to 40,000 people living in the surrounding villages.

At the dawn of the summer solstice, the "solstice post" and the central point of the wooden circle are perfectly aligned with the sun when it emerges above the Monk's mound. The main mounds in this archaeological site are part of this alignment.

The first European explorers in North America were amazed at the vastness of the continent. The small groups of Vikings and Basque fishermen who arrived on the northeast coast, and the first Spanish,

French and English explorers, barely altered thousands of years of indigenous culture. The first European settlements were small factories, missions, and colonies, and they were established as fortifications in the midst of a large undiscovered territory.

By raising their flags, the Europeans affirmed their dominion over these lands and, in just four centuries, completely deprived the indigenous peoples. Although some indigenous groups controlled the hunting and harvest areas, and all respected the boundaries of sacred places, none of them conceived of the land as lines drawn on a map, that is, as something divided, bought and sold. The colonizers endeavoured to impose this concept with relentless determination.

This European invasion was manifested in three forms: the physical occupation of the territory by the newcomers, the imposition of Christianity in a spiritual sense, and the introduction of material elements such as weapons and alcohol. The natives were displaced, deceived by treaties not fulfilled, subjected, in some cases destroyed, and exposed to alcohol, as well as confined in reserves. However, their culture was not annihilated, partly thanks to the influence of brilliant leaders. Traditional indigenous cultures survived and adapted to modernity.

The Great Basin

In the past, the Great Basin was a set of lakes surrounded by mountains and fed by the melting of glaciers from the last glacial period. However, after thousands of years of extremely hot summers, these ancient lake beds have turned into an arid rocky desert. Rivers flowing from the surrounding highlands flow into small alkaline lakes or simply get lost in the land.

Surviving in this dry and desolate region, with its vegetation composed of artemis, pine pines and enebros, has been a challenge. Small-sized hunting animals, such as squirrels, rats and Hares, which shelter among the rocks and feed on seeds, herbs and very little water, are abundant. As for deer and antelopes, they are scarce and rarely venture away from the shores of lakes and rivers, where they seek pasture. This homeless land has traditionally been home to hunting and gathering villages, such as the shoshona, ute and paiute.

In the more arid areas of the basin, communities spent most of the year moving around the desert in small family groups. Since no area produced enough food to sustain a sedentary life, there was no strong sense of territoriality. The houses were simple conical structures open at the top, built with rods or juncs and hunted and collected everything that the desert provided, from small hunting animals to pineapples and seeds, as well as insects and reptiles.

Because of food shortages, the shoshons and other groups in the arid areas followed the subtle rhythms of the desert to seize seasonal opportunities. In the spring, for example, terrestrial squirrels and marmots were still fat and slow after hibernation, making it easier to catch them. Thro the seasons, they hunted different animals and collected food, and in autumn they gathered to harvest pineapples and store them in pit for the winter. They also built corrals to catch antelopes and practiced rabbit hunting. This abundance of food was crucial to the winter survival and spiritual well-being of communities, which strengthened their tribal identity through shared ceremonies and activities.

In the utes region, where humidity was sufficient to support large hunting animals, such as alps and bison, and the paiutes of eastern Sierra Nevada watered meadows andined food reserves for longer.

However, the arrival of Europeans exerted a strong influence on the Great Basin and its inhabitants. The introduction of the horse around 1700 allowed the shoshons to expand into the plains and assimilate new traditions. When gold was discovered in California and western Nevada, the basin natives could not resist the advances of the white settlers, as they lacked warrior tradition and weapons to defend themselves. In 1863, the U.S. government took control of the region, and by 1874, most of the indigenous people had become either a wage labour force or were entirely dependent on the government.

Northwestern

In the northwestern region, natives of the Northwest Coast culture live in communities with spacious wooden houses. Thanks to a mild climate and the availability of abundant food, in particular salmon, they have the ability to devote a considerable amount of time to their rituals. Each clan has as its founding figure a mythical being, symbolized in totemic posts and other objects. Among these mythical beings, the Cuervo, the Ave Trueno and the Spirit Cannibal stand out.

The villages of the haidas

In the archipelago of Queen Carlota, located in British Columbia, is the land of the haids, known as Haida Gwaii, which means "the islands of the people". These are a proud maritime community that gets its wealth from the sea, and in the past, their villages were the most prosperous on the northwest coast. Before the arrival of Europeans in the 1770s, about 7,000 haidas lived in more than 30 coastal villages, consisting of solid houses built with cedar boards. Some settlements were small, while others spread along the coast, covering up to 1.5 km.

Similar to other houses in the northern northwestern region, the haida houses were spacious and rectangular, shared by several related families. These typical dwellings included corner poles, inner poles that held the roof beams, ceilings and cedar floors, all connected by wooden ropes or clavings. There were platforms along the inner walls for sitting and sleeping, with wooden divisions or cedar beams separating the different families.

The social hierarchy was reflected in the disposition of the families in the house, with the boss occupying the most distinguished place, at the far end of the entrance, and the slaves near the door. The traditional houses of the Haidas had a single central home, with few openings apart from the door and the hole in the roof where the smoke went out. Sometimes the door had the shape of a figure carved or painted on the façade or on a totemic poles.

This entry was a reflection of nature similar to a womb of housing. The villages were mainly occupied during the winter, as in the summer, the inhabitants moved to temporary camps to collect food as they developed.

If you looked at a haida village as it was in the 19th century, you would be amazed to see the set of carved cedar poles that rose between the houses of the haida villages. These indigenous peoples had more posts and greater height than any other group on the northwest coast. There were three main types: the totemic post, which showed the emblems of the families living in each house; the commemorative post, erected in honour of the ancestors and to whom tribute was rendered; and the mortuary post, on which the coffin containing the remains of the forefathers was placed.

In the late 19th century, European diseases and governmental and missionary resettlement programmes caused the depopulation and abandonment of many Haida villages.

By 1900, about a thousand surviving haidas were located in Massett and Skidegate, missionary settlements north of Queen Charlotte's archipelago. From 1890, the village of Yan became deserted. In 1991, the descendants of the last inhabitants of Yan gathered in the abandoned village to conduct a ceremony of erection of a new totemic post representing the bear clan. This cedar pole was carved by Jim Hart, a member of the new generation of indigenous artists who, over the past three decades, have dedicated themselves to the resurgence and preservation of the ancient sculpture skills of the northwest coast.

The unfortunately abandoned Haida villages soon deteriorated, as the white settlers cut the carved poles to use them as timber, sent them to museums or let them deteriorate.

The Great Plains

The Great Plains, which used to be the home of nomadic buffalo hunters, saw the development of the region's classical culture after the introduction of the horse and the influence of the peoples from the forests. In this culture, personal relationships with spirits play an important role, and myths reflect the importance of the gods of the elements and belief in a supreme being. Myths related to animals and institutions, such as the worship of the sacred pipe, are especially highlighted.

The interior of the North American subcontinent is characterized by vast plains and meadows extending from the southern forests of the ancient Canadian shield granite rock, in the north of Manitoba, Saskatchewan and Alberta, to the Texas Lowlands and the folded eastern cliffs of the Rocks that reach the Mississippi Valley. Amidst these vast plains, hills rise as isolated islands, such as the Black Hills, the Badlands of South Dakota and the Sand Hills of Nebraska. The river valleys, hidden until the prairie drops abruptly, provide vital resources such as water, trees, flora and fauna, and protection against the strong breeze winds.

In an earlier era, huge herds of animals, mostly bison (or buffalo), walked under the immense sky and survived from the plentiful grasses of the prairie. Since there were no natural barriers or significant predators, the bison prospered in millions. Humans initially settled near rivers and depended on valley resources, which included bears, deer, rabbits and hunting birds. They hunted bison on foot, often trapping them in barracks or pits.

Nearly a millennium ago, some groups moved to the plains, and nomadic bands began to settle in villages, turning the fertile plains created by river groves into cultivation areas. These cultures flourished until they came into contact with European colonizers. Climate change sometimes forced adaptations in villages' lifestyle, as droughts damaged corn crops. Also, villages sometimes had to relocate due to a shortage of wood to build shelters and light fireplaces, or due to occasional conflicts. The ancestors of the mandanes emerged in the middle valley of the Missouri River and, in the late 12th century, established contacts with the ancestor of the arikaras and pawnees, who migrated from the present-day regions of Nebraska and Kansas to escape the drought, leading to a fusion of cultures in the region.

At the arrival of the Europeans, most of the indigenous communities lived in large surrounded villages along the banks of the main rivers. The pawnees lived in Nebraska, the arikaras occupied much of what is today South Dakota, and the mandanes settled in North Dakota. These groups, known as "hortellans", were skilled farmers whose lifestyle followed a similar pattern: they planted in spring, hunted bison and harvested pre-winter during summer and early autumn.

Life in the plains underwent a significant change in the 16th century, when the Spaniards reintroduced the horse, a species that had extinct in North America thousands of years earlier. The first to use horses were the pawnees, and by the end of the 17th century, other tribes in the region followed their example. The farmers found that the use of the horse facilitated their seasonal bison hunting. Some tribes from forested regions, such as the Cheyenes, moved to the plains and became farmers, but with the introduction of the horse, they also became bison hunters. This increase in mobility and migration to the plains led to new rivalries for land and resources.

Tipi played a crucial role in adapting to a less sedentary lifestyle. This conical dwelling, originally conceived by the northern tribes of the forests, was perfectly adapted to the way of life in the plains. It was built with bison poles and skins, and could be quickly disassembled and transported into wooden structures pulled by horses.

In the 19th century, the plains became a mosaic of cultures. A southern Arapaho chief mentioned that he had been in contact with various tribes, including the Comanches, Kiowas, Apaches, Caddos, Pawnees, Crows, Gros-ventres, snakes, Osages, Arikaras and Nez percé, and that he communicated with them through the sign language, which in the past functioned as a kind of frank language in the region.

The incorporation of the horse into the Great Plains brought with it numerous benefits for the native tribes, although the weapons had a less positive impact. With access to these firearms, the northern Algonquin tribes and the Iroquois League expanded to the west in search of the fur trade. As a result of this pressure, in the early years of the 18th century, the Ojibwas displaced the Minnesota Sioux, forcing them to move towards the plains. The Sioux, in turn, confronted the Mandanes, the Arikaras and the Hidatsas along the Missouri River.

The horse revolutionized bison hunting, and by the mid-19th century, indigenous hunters had significantly increased the number of bisons hunted. However, when the white settlers joined the hunting, the bison population declined drastically, depriving the tribes of the Great Plains of one of their most essential natural resources.

The arrival of white settlements, war, diseases and the extinction of the bison marked the end of the traditional way of life of the plain tribes. Those peoples who had once wandered freely through vast lands were confined in reserves. In the Great Plains, resistance to the White invasion was stubborn, culminating in the tragic Wounded Knee massacre, in which about 200 lackeys lost their lives.

The jump of the bison

The hunting method known as "The Bison Jump" took advantage of the poor vision of these animals, since as herbivores of the plains, they did not need a sharp vision. This visual limitation proved to be beneficial to the indigenous peoples, especially before there were horses. The hunters guided the bisons towards a cliff or precipice, or directed them towards a natural barracks or artificial channel created with rocks and dirt.

When the bison finally perceived the obstacle, it was too late, and often dozens or even hundreds of them perished in a single stroke.

A place in Alberta called "Head-Smashed-In" was used for more than five millennia for this hunting practice, and houses the remains of hundreds of thousands of bison. The presence of complete skeletons and bones without meat reveals that sometimes more bisons were killed than needed to obtain food, skin and other products.

However, before the decline of its population in the 19th century, the number of bisons was so numerous that it could withstand excessive hunting.

Southwest

The southwest of the United States and Mexico is a region of arid beauty, carved by erosion over millions of years in plateaux, dusty plains, and deep canyons. In this vast territory, the tones of the earth, from red to black, are mixed with the stunning green of desert vegetation. Steep mountains and volcanic craters rise to the horizon, standing out against the intense blue sky. Life in this area is largely dependent on the scarce, but intense summer rains that temporarily revive the canyons and quickly absorb into the sand. Fluid rivers, such as the Grande to the east and the Colorado to the west, as well as the Salt and the Gila to the north of Mexico, pass through the rocky stretch.

The flora and fauna of this region are delicate and largely dependent on humidity. At high altitudes, pine trees and enebros cling to shallow soils between rocks and canyons, while in desert plains, bushes, cactus and mosques thrive, except in drier areas such as Death Valley, where extreme heat and drought are constant.

In this culture of desert regions are included the various Indians, people, so called for their sedentary life in villages. They share ideas derived from the mythology of the "emergence" and agriculture, and in their religion the masquerading personifications of mythic spirits are of great importance. Navajos and Apaches arrived in the region around 1400 and adopted elements of local myths and rituals.

Water scarcity has been a determining factor in the lives of the inhabitants of this region for thousands of years. Over time, populations have practiced harvesting and hunting according to the traditions of the desert, using all that nature provides as food, clothing and shelter. Some ancient groups even venture into agriculture, growing corn and shrimp, applying knowledge acquired from Mesoamerica. Agriculture flourished in this arid southwest, reaching an unusual level of development compared to other regions of America.

The success of these ancient desert farmers is reflected in their art, technology, and rituals, which were notoriously complex. The Mogollons, for example, lived in the mountains, building semi-buried houses that offered insulation against extreme temperatures. They cultivated a variety of foods, including corn, juveniles, shrimp, tobacco and cotton. His Mimbres ceramics are known for their impressive black and white geometric designs, as well as for figures of animals, human beings and other entities.

Around 1200 or 1400, the Mogollons were influenced by another desert civilization, the Anasazis, who originated around 100 BC between plateaux and canyons. The Anasazis cultivated on terraces and irrigation fields and lived in semi-buried houses. However, around 750, they introduced a completely new architectural style, building adobe houses with roofs of bars, grass and clay, supported by wooden beams.

They created large complexes or villages at the top of the plateaux and on the slopes of the canyons, with each floor a little further back than the lower one. The Pueblo Bonito complex, built in the Chaco Canyon around the year 900, has five floors and approximately 700 rooms.

The Anasazis left an impressive legacy of painted ceramics, multicolored fabrics, mosaics, jewelry adorned with turquoise, feathered garments and other ornamental elements. However, this civilization came to an end due to droughts that lasted over several generations. By 1300, the Anasazis abandoned their settlements and moved near the rivers or resumed a nomadic lifestyle, focused on hunting and harvesting.

During the period of the first Spanish incursions in 1539 and 1540, various indigenous groups with varying lifestyles were found in the region. Some lived in villages and practiced agriculture on the banks of rivers or on desert plains. These groups included the villages, the hopis, the zuni, the pimas and the O'odham tohonos. (papagos). Others, such as the Apaches and the Navajo, were nomads, engaged in hunting and harvesting. The Hopis inherited the Anasazi tradition and adapted it to the Colorado River region.

From Pueblo Oraibi, located at the top of the Black Table in Arizona, the hopis descended hundreds of kilometers down steep paths that serpented through cannons and cracks of limestone to the plain. There, they planted corn in sandy soils to take advantage of the underground moisture generated by summer storms. The women grinded the dried grain with smooth stones to make piki, a kind of corn flour bread, water and wood ashes that they boiled on an oily limestone. They also woven baskets with rabbit hair and zumaque branches and created pieces of alpha in a similar style to the Anasazis, decorated with elegant geometric designs in tones of red, brown and black on clear clay. The men collected, carved and threaded cotton, which the women dyed with the colors of the desert and used to make garments.

In the deserts watered by the Salt and Gila rivers, pimas continued to practice the way of life developed by another ancient people, the hohokam. These had built irrigation channels up to 16 km long to irrigate corn fields, juveniles, shrimp, tobacco and cotton planted in the desert. In the more arid lands of the highlands, groups such as the O'odham towns in the Sonora Desert harvested cactus, the saguaro, and hunted animals such as muflons, deer, ducks, goats, and rabbits.

The Apaches and Navajoes had more northern roots and spoke Atapascan languages similar to those of the natives of the far north of Canada and Alaska. Although the exact date of their arrival to the southwest is not known, in general terms, the Apachesined a nomadic lifestyle similar to their northern relatives, devoting themselves to hunting and harvesting. The Jicarilla Apaches of northern New Mexico learned agricultural techniques from nearby peoples, although they did not integrate into their cultures. They often came into conflict with the local peoples for the resources of the desert. On the other hand, the Navajo, before the domestication of sheep by the Spaniards, led a life of hunters and gatherers. Once they acquired sheep, they became skillful shepherds, developing skills in threading and weaving. Unlike the Apaches, the Navajo settled in scattered groups and adopted the desert as their home.

California

The southwestern end of North America is surrounded by mountains: coastal chains descend to the sea south of Baja California and to the east the majestic Sierra Nevada. The warm Pacific Ocean air throws moisture into California, irrigating fertile valleys and turning parts of the southeast, the Great Basin, and the Highlands into desolate, rocky slums. The people, finding the richness of this fertile environment irresistible, settled on the banks of the rivers, on the plains and on the coast. As the language mix shows, earlier immigrants came from many different places.

The coastal villages have fishing almost all year round. The Chumash people collected seafood from sandy beaches and fished tuna, plateaus, tuna, white tuna and other species. They entered the ocean in large board boats and hunted whales, foxes, sea lions, dolphins and marine nutries. Inland land, habitat of deer, rabbits and other minor hunting animals; Fish swim in rivers and streams, and the land produces a variety of wild plants that are used as food and medicine. The autumn harvest of bellots is decisive because they represent a basic food, mashed and washed with plenty of water, the bellots become a edible powder that is boiled to make strawberries or baked to make unleavened bread.

The Louisians who lived in northern Baja California had no difficulty gathering abundant land and water resources in the same territory, although for most Californians, the seasonal cycle was the only way: a longer return to the sea.

The sources of food are so clearly defined in time and space that the existence of hunting and harvesting is based on periodic rhythms closer to those of sedentary agricultural societies than those of the harvesters of the plains and forests of Noñe and Oriente. A group may be temporarily accommodated in secoya bark campaign shops. If he enters, he often takes with him the whole winter village, consisting of houses with columns and roofs of straw, and in each house many families live.

To some extent, each group has control over resource-rich lands. For example, the Chumash divided their hunting areas and those of other groups into key areas for wild plants, animal habitats and fishing. In some areas, several enlarged families united and established larger entities with defined territories, each of which was endowed with a main village and heads.

There was so much abundance that trade-off became a common practice. The hups exchanged with the yurok bellotas and other foods from the interior in exchange for algae, dished fish and secoya shelters. The Californians used certain forms of money - for example, the Dentalium shells - for trade, as a symbol of power and social status and as funeral objects.

The discovery of gold, in 1848, achieved what the Mexican and Spanish missions had failed to. Waves of settlers arrived to search for gold and explore the richness of the landscape. Although the Hupa survived thanks to the protection of the isolated river valley they occupied, the life of the Chumash, Louisians, Pomos and other peoples came to a brutal end.

The natives of California were skilled baskets. Both the male and female pomos produced vessels, squirrels, hats, and other objects that they cycled with typical geometric drawings, to which they frequently added feathers and shells.

Chaco Canyon

New Mexico's Chaco Wash remains dry most of the year, but recovers from storms, transporting rainwater streams from one place to another in the desert. Most of the water is absorbed by the soil, but the more eroded alluvial plains of the Chaco Canyon retain moisture and sustain agriculture. The Anasazi (Ancestrals), ancient farmers of the desert, lived in this region. Around 1020, the Anasazi began extensive construction in the Chaco Canyon to accommodate their prosperous agricultural population. The ruins of eight cities still remain in the canyon itself, with the ruin of a ninth city, Pueblo Alto, on the table to the north. In this area thousands of small ruins have been discovered, which today are of great archaeological interest.

Pueblo Bonito, the largest village, became an important center of turquoise treatment. Skilled workers obtained raw materials from distant mines and processed them to obtain polished stones that were then exchanged in Mexico. The resulting wealth is evident in the variety of exotic materials and items found in Pueblo Bonito, including copper bells, marine shells and dwarf feathers. Anasazi culture came to an abrupt end. In 1130, due to a great drought that lasted 60 years. With the loss of Chaco Wash's seasonal wealth, the Anasazi did not survive. 1,220 people left the city and were scattered in distant river valleys. The Chaco Canyon is now part of the Chaco National Cultural Historical Park. The largest city, Chaco Canyon, was called Pueblo Bonito and was an architectural wonder. From the outside, it looked like a fortress surrounded by semi-circular walls, huge and almost monotonous. But the walls encircle a high-rise complex with about 700 rooms that opens to a large square and was the largest residential complex built before the twentieth century. The square was occupied by two large circular kivas, each with a capacity for several hundred people. Both these rooms and the nearby 40 smaller rooms testify to the active spiritual life of the inhabitants of Pueblo Bonito. Some of the early Europeans who saw this population refused to believe it was the work of the ancestors of the present-day Indian people and attributed it to Mesoamerican civilizations such as the Toltecs and the Aztecs.

The northwest coast and plateau

Along the northwest coast, the western mountains descend to the sea. In places where there are no extensive islands on the coast that provide protection, the water slips through the high, tree-covered slopes, and the pressure rises through long flooded valleys and reaches the cold inner forests. Warm ocean currents flow between islands and coastal plains, generating abundant temperate rains surrounded by sand and slopes. On a dry plateau that stretches over mountains and fjords, coniferous forests are separated from the steep terrain by open meadows covered with artemis and splashed with oak. The scattered lakes and two large river systems, the Columbia and Fraser rivers, are fed by the water from the glacial meltdown that comes from the mountains.

People from these different landscapes depended on salmon. Adult and ripe fish flow upstream from the sea during the spring and move among the creeks of the river's submerged waters. Salmon was a source of food as predictable as seasons, and the only agriculture in the fertile river deltas and on the coast was the cultivation of scattered tobacco.

Despite the lack of salmon, the coast had a great deal of resources, such as trout, bacon, halibut, shrimp, eperlans and other fish. The oo-lichan, a small specimen, contains so much oil that they dried it, put a mecha on it and used it as a candle. Marine mammals also grew. All the villages hunted foxes, marsopes, sea lions and sea nutries, and the nootkas and makahs devoted themselves to whale fishing. The sites of ancient villages are distinguished by clusters of shells of many meters due to the abundance of strawberries, mejillons, sea rye and oysters. The nearby forests were filled with roots and fertile berries, as well as deer, castors, bears, martas and other small-hunting animals.

One of North America's most complex cultures arose from the overwhelming natural abundance. Red cedar wood, which is soft but sturdy, was the raw material. The two-water ceiling in the northern houses was built with wooden houses covered with cedar plates and a large parquet. They cut and painted the houses frequently. The houses in the south were larger, had roofed roofs and had little or no orna-ment.

Northern artists used heraldic stamps of surprisingly complex and peculiar styles to cut and paint posts, house facades, boats and house-hold utensils. Belief in the fundamental creative forces was expressed artistically through the "Totemic posts", especially among the Tlingi-tes, the Haidas and the Tsimshian. The artistic activity coincided with the classist tendency of much of the poor population of the northwest coast.

The material representation of social status was crucial in areas whe-re peoples were divided into nobles, plebeys and slaves. Individuals, families and clans exhibited and possessed representations of animal ancestors and other mythological figures. They defended the owner-ship of some names, titles, songs, dances and myths, as well as areas for fishing, hunting and collecting crustaceans. Fewer symbols related to social status were represented, and artists dedicated themselves to shaping religious objects in sectors where society was less stratified, as was the case with the salish and the chinook.

The inhabitants of the inland communities that lived along the Fra-ser and Columbia river systems were hunters and gatherers, and their diet included fish, deer, alms, mossons, rabbits and other small-hun-ting animals, as well as plants from meadows and forests. However, they did not completely separate themselves from the cultures of their embryo. It is possible that barge canoes were introduced by the Pacific Coast culture since antiquity, as evidenced by stone sculptures of figures and animals. In recent times, organizations such as the nez percé have verified that the horse is perfectly adapted to the pastures of the plateau.

Potlatch

In communities where each person had a social category and trait, residents demonstrated their material wealth by giving a part or burning it in a potlatch ceremony. Sometimes, the leader of a clan or other nobility welcomed hundreds of guests with impressive dances and abundant banquets. Items presented or burned in the fireplaces included fabrics, leather, dresses, baskets, utensils, counts, and canoes. The wealth at stake was really impressive.

Potlatch was traditionally celebrated to celebrate events such as birth, puberty, marriage, inheritance and death. The clan showed during the potlatch its material wealth, its strength and its connection with the past. Each music, dance, image and dress symbolized the heritage and vitality of the clan.

With the arrival of European merchandise, the festivals reached their peak and on one occasion thirty-three thousand blankets were presented. Potlatches became so popular that in 1885 the Canadian government banned them as anti-progressive waste at a time when traditional life was under pressure.

They were carried out in secret until in 1950, the ban was removed.

Cedar

Previously, the islands and mountainous slopes of the Pacific coast were filled with red cedars due to heavy rains. The ripe red cedar was a thin giant whose compact trunk was covered above the thick malice, unlike the firm, upright and sober Douglas and the naked madroño. The cut cedar bark was a valuable source of fibers for weaving a wide range of items, such as baskets, ropes, rods, coats and other garments.

Cedar wood is not only soft and easy to work, but also extremely elastic and resistant to wet weather and salty sea air. The carefully carved totem cedar poles survived the villages in which they were built. Occasionally, they removed large cedar trunks, enlarged the central area by using steam and stretching, and then knitted them to create aerodynamic offshore canoes. The Laidas reached a length of 21 meters. The carpenters reproduced the complex pictorial styles of the northwest coast on cedar wood panels and converted wooden blocks into spectacular masks and precious ceremonial basins.

The cedar fiber is so soft that long and thin bars and tablets can be easily manufactured. This made cedar an ideal material for the construction of large community houses that were found in abundance in the region. Cedar was also used to create "folded wooden boxes", which were created by casting steam on a cedar plate and shaping it to give it the desired shape.

Sub-Arctic

A large forest surrounded by countless lakes, ponds, streams and rivers stretches north of the northeastern meadows and forests and around Hudson Bay.

In rocky and infertile soils, resilient pine trees, piceas, and oaks can survive, and in protected areas, trembling oaks, sauces, and beetles can withstand long and terribly cold winters. Liquids and mosses cling to trees, stones and soil everywhere. To the west, the forest turns into cold tundra. Although the sub-Arctic summers become warm, the nearby tundra and forests are not a good season because there are many mosquitoes, mosquitos and other insects that bite in the air. The soil remains frozen at all times due to the thin layer melted by the sun.

Most of the people who lived in this desolate territory devoted themselves to hunting, fishing and going out in small family groups to find food.

The villages east of the Rockies, such as the Chipewyan, the Dogrib, the Kutchin (gwich'in) and others, used the Atapascan language. The Algonquin-speaking peoples, such as the Cris, the Ojibwas, the Naskapis and the Montagnais, lived in the granite landscape devastated by glaciers that surrounded the Hudson Bay and extended eastward to the Atlantic.

The prey was the target of hunter groups. To ensure fish supply, they lived on the shores of the lakes during the winter and built blankets or small tipis. In addition, they could move on foot using rackets or on trolleys and tobogans. Some groups knew the locations of hunting and family traps and returned there every year for hunting, fishing or gathering. Catching animals such as caribou, alce and others that left footprints on the snow was easy. In canoes made of beetle bark, they traveled rivers and lakes while the spring dew crushed the land.

Caribou and reindeer were the main food for life in the northern subarctic region. All parts of these animals were used by the peoples for different purposes, such as caribou leather types and tools and weapons made with bones and cornments. Although the caribou spends winter in small groups on the borders of tree vegetation, in early spring they migrate to the reproductive areas of the tundra, which extends to the north. They return to the south with their offspring during the short northern summer. During the journey, they are attacked by wolves and, at the intersections of rivers, humans put them in danger.

In addition, they were dedicated to the hunting of animals such as alces, almizclerous oxen, deer, animals with fur such as castors, visons, hares and nutries, as well as bison in the forests that were located to the north of the plains. There were Rocky Goats in the mountains of the western Yukon and Alaska. Pork spines lived in the forests and provided meat and puffs for dying, flattening, and adorning clothing and accessories. Non-domesticated birds increased in number. In the southern forests, the most common vegetable foods were berries, roots, wild rice and the soft inner crust of the algae. The northernmost Chipewyan lived mainly on meat and fish. Despite isolation and difficulties, the northern groups managed to maintain family ties, exchange wives, gather to organize caribou hunting expeditions and establish connections through the trade of metals such as copper, silicone and quartzite, which were essential for the creation of tools.

Sub-Arctic women are experts in hunting small animals. They are also traditionally engaged in peeling the caribou, pleasing the skins, peeling and preparing the meat.

CULTURES, CUSTOMS, WORLDVIEW

Sacred History

Western anthropology uses the term "mythology" to refer to stories that explain the interactions between the natural and the supernatural. Native Americans prefer to refer to "sacred history" because in popular culture, the term "myth" refers to "fiction". The stories that tell the history of the earth, the origin of the people and the life of ancestors and sacred beings are very real to many indigenous people. The landscape has been marked by these figures and the important events of their time, which are strongly remembered in the painted and carved images, as well as in the songs, dances and stories.

Some cultures believe that the earth was formed from the union of cosmic giants, while others believe that a small animal extracted it from the infinite ocean.

The great heroes, supernatural beings who often took animal form, often appear in the accounts of the difficulties of the early humans. These heroes provided light and fire or protected the people from the destroyers or helped them on their long and difficult journey from their place of origin to their homeland. Dangers also wore in the form of unpredictable timers that caused problems with their tracks, although they also contributed to creating today's world.

The First American Peoples

The sacred beings claim that North America has never been an uninhabited territory. It came to life when the first human beings came to the surface, coming from other worlds that were inside the Earth's womb or from parallel worlds which existed beyond the sky. Each group, whether they lived on the rocky shores, on the extensive and almost infinite prairie, in the forests of the northeast or in the deserts of the southeast, had a spiritual homeland where the people saw the proof of their origins.

Archaeologists studying the foundations of early American cultures have found remains of homes, animal bones and fine stone tools dating back more than 10,000 years. They were left by hunters whose ancestors brought mammots and other large animals from the last glacial

period from Asia to America. At that time, the sea level dropped significantly, leading to the union of the present-day regions of Siberia and
Alaska by a land language known by experts as Beringia.

It is possible that groups of hunters crossed Beringia without res-
trictions before the sea covered it again. Although hunters gradually
arrived in America around 8000 BC, humans had established their presence virtually throughout the continent.

Historical Records

The North American Indians had no writing and almost all of the
story was transmitted orally through narrators who used non-technical
rules to remember often complex details. However, this does not mean
that the Indians lacked a method of recording historical events. Several
groups in the plains used the "winter computing" mode of permanent
archiving. Every year, almost always during the cold season, they painted a symbol or a realistic figure in a large-sized, specially processed
bison skin to commemorate the most important event that affected the
community that year.

According to the set-t'an calendar of the kiowas of 1882, the sacred
being Patepte tried to recover the herds of bison that quickly disappeared from the plains at that time.

On the calendar you can see a wizard sitting in the sacred place,
dressed in a red ceremonial blanket, surrounded by eagle feathers and
with a bison next to him.

Although it could vary, the arrangement of the winter computing
images was almost always in the form of a spiral, with the oldest image
located in the center. Some skins have a tribal history of more than two
centuries. Only a few record the constant succession of events, and the
people carried the count of winter to the extent that they were able to
refer to the facts they represented.

Animals from the southwest, such as maricops, pimes, and O'odham toons (papages), indicated the advance of time by creating symbols on the flat side of the "calendar sticks", which were wooden strips
of about a meter in length. Each symbol represented a specific event
for a specific year, which was remembered by the "conserver of the
calendar sticks", an expert in the same position as the healers, singers,
and alpharers. Each year a new symbol was created during the harvest season. Conservatives in each community exchanged information,
allowing them to be informed about events that occurred outside their

immediate surroundings.

The older members of the tribe could accurately identify the date of birth thanks to the accuracy of the sticks. Like winter calculations, the effectiveness of frames as historical documents depended on the memory of people. From time to time, Conservatives were sold to death, but the most common way to do so was to eliminate them.

In the northeast, the most significant events were used to be grouped into shell counts. The conservatives of these belts kept in their minds the details of the documented events. They were used as documents to keep treaties, such as the one established by the Iroquois League.

Walum Olum was a pictorial record of the northeastern lenni-lena-pes (delawares). He painted in the bark of a tree and described more details than others, but still depended on the memory of a skilled narrator. The ceremonial narratives lasted weeks and required a great effort of memory on the part of the narrator to remember the events represented. A fragment that talks about the period of contact with the Europeans, spanning from approximately 1600 to 1818, is still preserved.

The Earth

Native identity has always been centred on the earth. The Indians had a close connection with the physical world, as did other peoples, especially those living in tribal societies. This was reflected in their actions to search for plants, sew prey, cut trees, tear land, cross the forest or cross a field. The structure of indigenous life and the characteristics of Indian cultural expression were more than anything influenced by the inevitable natural rhythms of the specific environments in which they lived.

The relationship between the Indians and the landscape, however close it may be, is an easy peculiarity to alter or break. The drought forced the ancient Anasazi to abandon their luxurious cities and settle in simpler places. The introduction of weapons and horses by the white in the plains and surrounding areas established new connections between the hunter peoples and the hunting territories. However, these changes were more gradual than the traumatic breakdown caused by the arrival of white settlers to the west in the 19th century and the expulsion of Indians from their traditional territories. Despite all this, the lives of the Aborigines continued, as always, to be determined by what each people took from the land and gave in return.

Origins of Mythology

Myths about the activities of the gods are the most important from a spiritual point of view, especially those about the creation of the universe and man, the origin of death, animals and plants like corn and tobacco.

Only at specific times of the year and in special situations, people told these myths. The whole-year myths were more of entertainment or education, they were told as moral lessons and fun, so they were more adaptable in their interpretation and elaboration.

All the tribes believed that everything that moved was alive. For animists, there is always a being hidden in every stick, stone, tree and animal, and any object can easily be transformed: the young woman hiding under the moon is transformed into a mound of earth and a candle, into a rock, a hammer, a tent hanging, a hair or a grain of earth. Each object has its own existence and can act according to its own will.

This form of understanding arose as a direct expression of human powerlessness before the mysterious, powerful and terrible forces of nature.

Fear caused them to attribute supernatural powers to natural phenomena, as they depended entirely on it. They can confront natural objects and overcome them; they can offer sacrifices and ask for their protection. The smallest can be used as amulets. If used on the body, these amulets or spirits of objects, such as a bear or bear's tail, a piece of a buffalo horn or a morse hook, can protect against hostile forces.

In such precarious conditions, life would have been plagued with constant fears due to the lack of protection against evil spirits. The sortileges, songs and sacrifices, as well as the recitation of myths, gave hope to overcome the forces of destiny.

Creation Stories

The dramas of Native American stories about how it began to exist are represented by characters in contexts that fit the environment in which they developed. Creation accounts include humans, animals, and supernatural beings in human or animal form. Human experiences, such as sexual union, separation, great strength tests, and long and difficult journeys, serve as the basis for cosmic events.

The narratives are transmitted through oral tradition and sacred persons, narrators and aboriginal scholars recreate them in each narrative and often incorporate new elements acquired through dreams, visions and current experiences. The teachings of Christianity and the pan-Indian religious movements have influenced them over the last five centuries, presenting powerful metaphors about the beginnings of the world.

Some stories say that the gods created the world in an empty report. In the Apache stories, the Black Wind created the earth, the Yellow Wind gave it light and other deities collaborated to create landscapes and life forms. Other groups of people believe that the world has always existed and that at first it was a plain without characteristics and submerged in darkness until a great spirit intervened. For the Californian shasts, Chareya (the old man from above) lived in the heavenly world, but made a hole in the sky and fell to the ground on a pile of ice and snow. The sun came out of the hole, melted the ice and formed the sea, the lakes and the rivers. Chareya planted trees and created birds from their leaves. The Iroquois myth of creation also mentions the fall of the sky.

Sex intervenes in some stories about the origins. According to an Inuit creation account, two men escaped the great universal flood and married. The "wife" man's penis broke when she became pregnant, which turned her into a woman and gave birth to her first child.

Many Native Americans today see Mother Earth as a living essence. It is likely that for most tribes it is a relatively new idea (i.e., after the encounter with the Europeans), but for others it goes back to a rather old tradition. For example, according to the people of the Salish linguistic family, who live in the interior of British Columbia, the great Old Spirit created the earth from a woman. The woman in question is mouth-up and people live on her. The trees and the grass are his hair, the ground is his flesh, the rocks are his bones, and the wind is his breath. Winter is when it's cold and summer is when the weather is hot. Every time it moves, there's an earthquake.

Traditionally, Indians have sought sacred images, voices and facts from the time when things began to exist in the landscape and animals. They often claim that known animals play an important role in the process of creation, as in the accounts that include the "diver of the earth". This myth is present all over the world and corresponds to a heroic narrative of creation. In several indigenous cultures of the United States, the earth is in a state of infinite, watery chaos in which there is no firm ground. One being asks several animals to collect mud and dive to the bottom of the ocean. In the end, someone succeeds and with the recovered soil forms a solid soil. These living beings are known as "land divers" and are sometimes considered small and humble heroes. The scuba diver in the cherokee tale is a water scabbard, while for the chickasaw it is a river crab and for the cheyenes it's a foul.

The narratives of land divers are more common among the hunting and gathering peoples due to the rich and profound relationships they maintain with the animals of the forests, deserts and meadows. Other agricultural groups, such as the Iroquois, also share this tradition, indicating that the history goes back to before the adoption of the agricultural lifestyle.

According to other creation accounts, the first humans sprang up from the ground, as did crops. These versions are more common in agricultural tribes, such as rural communities in the southwest. In these myths, the struggle for survival generally takes the form of a large migration across several worlds to the present. According to the caddo narrative of the origins, Luna, the first man, created thousands of people in a single village from a world dominated by darkness and, with the help of Timer Coyote, led them through a hole to the present world. Many people lost their way to the fatherland of the caddies and became the ancestors of other tribes. Those who stayed with the Moon settled in a place called Highwood on the Top of the Hill and, along with the first man, Coyote and other beings, gradually became the tribe of the Caddies. Over time, the people who separated during the journey spoke different languages, although in the origins all spoke Caddo.

For most North American Indians, the landscape preserves the memory of important events so that they can always identify. For example, the tewa world is surrounded by four mountains and four sacred hills, in the center of which is the hole from which humans are believed to have come out. The sacred place of exit is represented by a hole in the floor of the kiwa (ceremonial chamber).

In Chaco Canyon, New Mexico, there is the great canyon of Chetro Keti, one of the settlements of the ancient Anasazi. The Kivas remain the center of the traditional ritual life of the Hopis and other Southwest Indian peoples. The ceremonial cameras of the hopis use a soil depression called sipapu to recall the hole through which the first humans came to the world in the history of hopis creation.

Myths of Creation

The most well-known creation myth, tells about an animal looking for mud in the bottom of the sea. The earth arises from the sand that the duck (or the raven, pigeon, fox, vison, eagle and halcon) carries on its peak. In a Cheyenne myth, it is said that the back of Grandma Tortoise is where the earth rests.

The accounts of the flood are related to the story of the divers in search of land, due either to the torrential rains or to the tears of those of the upper world who weep for the evil acts committed on the earth.

Most myths describe mankind as made of clay (hopi) or grass, feathers, sticks or corn pans. Man can be created from the bones of the dead, from the sweat of the Creator, or simply as a result of a desire.

In some tribes, the gods marry each other: Mother Earth with Father Heaven, the Sun with the Moon, the Dawn Lucero with the Eve. The first being was a woman, according to the Iroquois and Hurons of the northeast, and the Navajo of the southwest.

Eastern Canadian micmac sees creation as a constant flow. The world beneath the earth, the world under the water, the earth world, the spirit world, and the world above the earth and the heavenly world are the six worlds that make up his universe. Reality fluctuates according to people's preferences and never remains stable.

Features of Wakan Tanka

For the Lakotas, J. is the supreme being according to Wakan Tanka, the "Great Mystery". The myth of the creation of this people says that the higher gods, each of whom has an aspect of Wakan Tanka, felt alone and created other manifestations of the god. The Lakotas use the word "Father" to refer to any of these individual aspects and "Grandfather" for transcendent deity in their prayers.

The higher gods first created the related gods (the Moon, the Fugitive Star and the Thunderbird), and then the related Gods: Bípedos (who were relatives of humans and bears), Buffalo, Four Winds, and Torbellino. The fourth group, that of god-like beings, has to do with the soul, the spiritual essence and the sacred powers: Nagi (shadow or ghost of the dead), Nagila (like a shadow), Niya (life or breath) and Sicun. (poder espiritual).

Wakan Tanka consists of these four groups of four aspects, also known as Tob Tob ("Four-Four"), which is expressed through its 16 aspects but is larger than their sum.

Wakan Tanka			
Higher Gods	Associate Gods	Similar Gods	Similar to the gods
Sun, Sky, Rocky, Earth	Moon, Wind, Shooting Star, Thunder bird	Bipeds, Buffalo, Four Winds, Whirlwind	Nagi Nagila Niya Sicun

Creation Myths: The Earth Diver

Many cultures have myths about the Earth Diver in which the turtle plays an important role.

The cheyene account contains all the essential elements:

Maheo, known as the "All Spirit", created the Great Water, aquatic beings and birds, who were tired of flying and used to dive to find food. They could not do so until the focha tried, but when he returned, he dropped in Maheo's hand a small clay ball that he was carrying in his tip.

The Great Mother Turtle could only carry her after Maheo rubbed her in her hands. The first earth was formed when the clay continued to grow on his back.

Myths of creation: the great spirit.

Although North American cultures are very diverse, there are very few myths about the creation of the world. Most indigenous cultures believe that the universe was created by a supreme deity or the "Great Spirit".

This being is very revered, known as Gitchi Manitú among the Algonquins of the northeastern forests and Wakan Tanka among the Lakotas of the plains, but is too passive and too indefinite to consider him a different personality. In most cases, its only function is the creation of more precise figures, such as the Mother Earth and Father Heaven, very broad deities, or the Sun and Moon, to which other acts of creation are attributed when the supreme god withdraws to heaven. These figures can also be used as tools for human creation.

In most creation narratives, animal characters are presented as active entities: for example, it is told in scattered areas of the west that the Spider woven a fabric that eventually formed the earth. However, the most popular myth is that of the Earth Diver, who in many cases is a humble man who approaches the bottom of the primordial sea and collects the sand that, as it expands, forms the earth. A turtle, a common character in forest mythology, holds the world. This type of myth has parallels in Eurasia, as do the accounts of a great flood that appear in some versions of the creation myth, indicating that it may have migrated to the east.

The myth of the creation of the lakotas

The Lakota myth about creation begins with Wakan Tanka, the supreme being, whose spirit was in Inyan, the first god. There was only one, Han. (Black of Darkness). Inyan intended to demonstrate his abilities, however, not finding anything to use them, he created the goddess Maka (the Earth) and the blue waters with his blood. From these waters emerged the great Skan vault (Heaven), whose edge defined the limits of the earth. Skan used his energy to create the earth's darkness with Han and the waters with Inyan, and he himself created Wi (the Sun), whom he ordered to shine, causing the global warming. The four gods, Skan, Inyan, Maka, and Wi, met, and Skan the most powerful of them, said to them, "Al we are four, we have one origin, Wakan Tanka, which no one can understand, not even the gods themselves." He is a god of the gods.

The Creation of the World

The Awonawilona world, which contains everything, was hidden in darkness and emptiness. Fogs and streams emerged from Awonawilona, then the Sun formed an igneous ball that scratched the fogs and joined together to form drops of rain that became the ocean. Awonawilona then planted her seed in the ocean, and grew up to form a green cloak that spread across the sea. Then Awonawilona was divided into two parts: one was Mother Earth and the other was Father Heaven.

Mother Earth slipped over the sea with her fingers until she formed foam. It breathed over this foam and formed black and white fogs floating over the ocean like clouds. Father Heaven blown over the clouds and the rain began to fall on the earth.

Then Father Heaven ascended to heaven. Inside Mother Earth, life expanded rapidly and soon gave rise to the creation of living beings, starting with ugly snakes, passing through scary monsters and finally giant twins that emitted thunders opening large holes in the ground.

In order for men to escape from the dark entrances of the earth, climbers and climbing women built a rope staircase with trees and grasses. The soil was already plowed and ready to receive the first corn seeds when they managed to climb. People began to cultivate and harvest the harvest.

This is a story of the indigenous colonization of Arizona and New Mexico, the desert areas of southwest America.

Myth of the creation of navajos

The most extensive groups of native peoples in North America are the Navajo and their relatives, the Apaches, who now live in Arizona, New Mexico, and Utah, with about 160,000 people. His customs include the most complete narration of the myth of Creation, which consists of four stages.

1. The first stage, The Beginning, tells how the first men came to earth from the underworld.

2. The second stage, the Age of the Animal Hero, describes how the earth was ordered and the adventures of its first inhabitants.

3. The third stage, the Divine Age (Yei, directed by the Speaking God), tells the killing of monsters.

4. The fourth stage tells the birth of the Navajo nation and its first migrations.

Mythology of the Navajo

Today, more than 160,000 Navajo from Arizona, New Mexico and some areas of Utah are the most numerous Native Americans. The Apaches, as well as their close cousins and neighbors, probably arrived in the region before the year 1300.

Apart from some ancient and now declining myths of hunting, the Navajo mythology reflects the influence of the agricultural societies of some Indian peoples, such as the Hopis, from whom the myth of the "emergence" and much of its symbolism derives. Most of the Navajo mythology comes from the story of creation-emergence and several ceremonial myths, which are descendants of the latter.

Ceremonial myths mention heroic figures who are wounded or missing and seek the gods to recover. After reaching his goal and having learned the healing ceremony, the hero returns to his home to teach it and then moves to live with the gods.

A unique ceremonial myth speaks of two twins of a knife girl and the deity Yei, also known as the Speaking God. The children always leave the house and one day they are overthrown by a crumbling of rocks, leaving the greatest blind and the smallest dumb. They become a burden for their poor family and are asked to leave. That's how they go and look for the gods. The gods welcome them and prepare a healing ceremony in the sweat pavilion (a kind of sauna), where the speaking God helps them and reveals to them that he is their father. The boys shout of joy as healing is carried out, breaking a taboo by speaking in the sweat pavilion. Everything disappears and returns to its original state. He makes an offering to calm the gods, who heal them and make them as beautiful as their brothers. After returning home, they teach others the healing ritual and then go to become spirits that protect the animals and the storm.

Chippewas Myths

The Chippewa, a native Algonquin-speaking community living in the Great Lakes region, survive by hunting, fishing and harvesting, as well as growing corn and shrimp in the summer, collecting wild rice in the autumn, and extracting sugar from the arches in the spring. This cycle was characterized by a nomadic or semi-nomadic lifestyle. They quickly built dome-shaped shops called wigwams. In winter, they traveled their routes on foot or in canoe canoes, or using tobogans.

Chippewa myths can be divided into the following categories: the creation of Wenebojo (a real person); the accounts of Matchikwewis and Oshkikwe, in which women explain how to behave girls; the windigo accounts, where struggles between people and cannibals giants appear; the stories of animals, where real encounters of people with animals appear and anecdotes about animal tricks; and

The ritual of the Healing Dance was part of the Wenebojo cycle. Only during the winter were other stories told. Some said that frogs and snakes could not tell stories because they were evil spirits and should not hear them.

The Pacific Northwest Transformer

At first, the earth was flat, full of cannibal monsters and without mountains or trees. Then came the Transformator. The qhilleute say it was the sharp, intelligent eye; the makah say it is the horn; and the people of Puget Sound say it's the fox. The Chehalis believe it was the Moon that became a human, while the Tillamook represent her as a woman.

The tribes of Alaska in the north and the Rocky in the east use different expressions to refer to the Transformer.

The Transformator's camp had inexhaustible streams and springs.

The mountains were lifted up by him. Downloading a bag of wooden furs like those used by people for hair, he built the rocky cliffs of the quiet coast. The Sun was stolen from the greed that protected it and thrown into the sky.

The historical migration of the hopis

According to the hopis, the first people migrated upwards, crossed three commandos and reached the fourth world. The guardian spirit, masaw, suggested that they move north, south, east, and west to reach the sea, and then stop until they reach their common homeland. The journey was not completed by all the clans; some remained in the tropics and others lost their course. The returnees portrayed the migrations with two kinds of spirals: the square, which represents the return of the seas, and the round, which shows how they walked closer and closer to their home. The travels of the village form a large cross called Tuwanasavi (the center of the universe), whose epicenter is located in the present homeland of the hopis.

The creation of the Matacus Indians

For a long time, the sky has been above the earth and the earth below, where the winds, the clouds and each level has its inhabitants, connected by a large tree that connects the different worlds. The side of abundance was the cup of the tree. Human beings on Earth headed there to get food, moving forward and down on this "tree of life."

They did not comply with their customs of solidarity and did not offer the best to those who had difficulty climbing the big tree. The elders shouted and the Great Fire destroyed everything. Some of them, in the form of stars or constellations, wander through the Milky Way along with their ancestors.

Others escaped by entering under the ground and then coming out through the holes that the squirrels made. Together, they ejaculated in a cabbage ham. At one point, they realized that part of what they caught or fished was disappearing for no apparent cause. The gavel informed them of the arrival of strange beings from heaven. Hence, humans caused a drop of arrows and some of these strange celestial beings embedded themselves in the earth. The traitor pulled them out through his nails. These beings had two dented mouths, one in the middle of their face and the other in the center of their bodies, using both to consume the stolen food.

The beings approached the fire that was lit by the men because of the cold, but the eagle threw them a stone that dropped all the teeth of the lower mouth except one, which was the clitoris, since they were women. Since then, boys and girls have been the result of the union of men and women. Men have earthly power, while women have heavenly power.

Great snowfall in the north

A long time ago, one night, everything became very dark and it started to snow. It snowed all night and it seemed like it would never end. The snow began to cover the plants and bushes, making it difficult to find food for the animals, resulting in the death of many of them.

The council finally made the decision to send messengers to the sky to find out the reason behind the long night and snow. Each family of animals, birds and fish that lived on the shores of the Great Slave Lake received one member, and those who could not fly were carried on the back of those who were able. Each of them entered through a trap that led them into the Heavenly World.

A large store built of deer skins was next to the trampoline. The Black Bear lived in that place. There were some curious bags hanging from the roof. On consulting what was inside, they were informed that there were winds, one rainy bag and another cold; however, Black Bear refused to reveal what was in the last bag.

The curious animals untied the last bag and threw it through the trap down to the ground when Bear came out. The bag contained the sun, the moon and the stars, and the rays of the sun began to melt the snow.

The animals embarked on the return flight thinking that the world on earth was already safe. Some incidents occurred along the way: a castor broke his tail and stained the lynx with blood; the fist of the alce flattened; and the buffalo had a fist in his back.

The friendly and quiet life of the lake disappeared. When the flood waters withdrew, the fish realized that they could not live on land because birds and animals ate them, so they took refuge in the trees. Each animal chose his favorite place.

Soon, animals like birds and fish ceased to communicate with each other. Shortly thereafter, the first humans visited the lake. There has never been peace since then.

This story goes back to the slave tribe on the coast of the Great Slave

Lake in the Northwest Territories of Canada.

Origin of dry land

A common reason for divers' intervention is that several animals attempted to dive to the bottom of the great ocean to obtain sand or other materials for land to emerge.

In this story there are many animals and fish.

The (successful) duck, eagle, falcon, horn, and colibri are some of the tribes found in southern California. The coushatta tribes of Texas believe that the river crab is the only animal that achieves it after the frog and the castor failed to.

The myth of the twins and the origin of man, but instead of bringing land with its pinches, as other tribes report, the crab built a clay chimney that eventually reached the surface of the water.

North America. The Iroquois tribes

In the origins of the world, a woman pregnant with twins fell through a hole from the upper world where she lived to our world, which at that time was a desert. A twin came out of her mother's body with such force that it caused her death, thus revealing the wickedness of her spirit. His brother had a generous soul and devoted himself to the breeding of animals and plants.

The evil brother tried to follow his example, but only created reptiles and man, who was rectified by the good and gave him soul. The wicked man asked his brother who would be the king of the world, and he lost. From then on, he was destined to rule over the dead and remain as a spirit of evil for all eternity.

The Origins of Humanity

The creation of the first human beings is generally attributed to one or more deities, who also created the rest of the world. According to the Pauni, Tirawa, the main deity, asked the deities of the Moon and the Sun to join together to create the first human being, and also the Eve and Morning Stars, from which the first woman was born. Some Southeast peoples believe that the gods Mother Earth and Father Heaven were created by the supreme deity to give rise to the first living beings, including humans.

The hopis believe that two twin deities first created animals and then humans with clay, and gave them life by singing a ritual song.

According to the Iroquois and Forest Hurons, the first human ancestor was a woman named Ataensic, daughter of the Heavenly People, gods who descended to the earth, and the Navajo also believe that human beings come from a woman.

The "emergency" stories of the indigenous people and other inhabitants of the plains clearly show how humans came to the world today. Myths present the earth as a fertile mother and all-powerful breeder for people, animals and plants (como el hopi). This reflects the concerns of an agricultural society.

Stories contain an implicit morality, as humans are often forced to ascend to the higher world as a result of their bad actions. In some interpretations, these transgressions lead to the destruction of the underground worlds, where there are barely any living beings. From the point of origin, humans have evolved to their present habitats.

According to the source of the myth, humans are guided to the higher worlds by the Maize Mother or Spider Woman (both deities symbolize the earth), twin deities or heroes, and eventually reached the fourth world. The guardian spirit, masaw, suggested that they move north, south, east, and west to reach the sea, and then stop until they reach their common homeland. The journey was not completed by all the clans; some remained in the tropics and others lost their course. The returnees portrayed the migrations with two kinds of spirals: the square, which represents the return of the seas, and the round, which shows how they walked closer and closer to their home. The travels of the village form a large cross called Tuwanasavi (the center of the universe), whose epicenter is located in the present homeland of the hopis.

The origin of corn

There are a variety of myths about the origin of corn, which is the most important cereal in the diet of Native Americans. The Florida mikasuquis combine two very common concepts: the role of two brothers or heroes and the creation of something from another being.

Two brothers lived with their grandmother, and one day, tired of eating meat, they asked for something different. During that time, when they returned from hunting, Grandma offered them corn that they thought was delicious. However, because the grandmother refused to reveal her origin, the youngest spied on her on one occasion when she entered the barn and was surprised to see that she obtained the corn by rubbing the sides.

The grandmother understood that the brothers knew her secret when they rejected the cereal that night. He told them they would have to leave them forever, but that they would continue to live in the corn that grew on his grave.

Animals

Respect for animals.

Aboriginal Americans believe that human-animal relationships are deep and complex. Many peoples believed that animals were their direct descendants or, at least, were related to animals. As a result, they have the same rights and deserve the same respect as other human beings. Firstly, their willingness to sacrifice their lives to ensure the survival of humanity must be honoured.

Alaska's koyukons are aware that humans hunt them to survive and don't hurt them. However, they claim that, whether persecuted or not, they must be treated with humanity at all times. Every day it must be fed to a hungry dwarf that has been trapped in the snow until it recovers the necessary forces to come out on its own foot and get away. The koyukones believe that the animal and its soul are one. The spirit is peculiar to the animal in question, but it is also part of the collective spirit of the species, which means that all members of the kind can move away from the hunter if an individual is offended.

The fate of the hunter is influenced by hundreds of rules and taboos related to the proper treatment of animal spirits. They consider luck to be a powerful link between humanity and animal spirits. The koyukons honor the animals by respecting the rules because, otherwise, luck could abandon them, at the risk of the people not surviving. Boasting about something that hasn't happened yet can have the opposite effect; for example, by claiming that you will catch many castors, you suddenly realize that you can't catch a single specimen. The person who exaggerates his skills during the "bear hunt" may be devoured by this animal.

The white castor ritual of the chawi group of the pawnees honored the animals at an important moment in their lives: when they came out of hibernation. They believed that after winter, the gods gave life to animals. In the event that the corresponding ritual was carried out, a part of the divine power was granted to the doctors, who used it for the benefit of the population. Doctors were primarily responsible for carrying out the ritual, making them the third category of pawnees, after chiefs and priests.

The conservative of the white castor prepared the altar and chimney in his shelter when the animals began to move in January. In the company of another doctor, they set fire to the sacred pipe and exhaled in tribute to the animals. During a secret ceremony to purify the castor, they asked their closest relatives to bring meat to the shelter.

After a four-day period, a complex ceremony began in which doctors instilled life into the animals smoking in their honor. Each individual said, "Father, my current situation is of poverty." Have compassion on me. I need your help to heal sick people. It takes the disease away from our community, it offers valuable gifts and a long life.

Origin of animal qualities

Animals are often the main characters in American stories and sometimes appear as invented cosmic agents. The animals had leaders and counselors and lived in cabins or shops like the tribes. Animals interact with people and speak their language frequently.

Each animal embodies specific traits and characteristics. Almost always, the rabbit is cunning and cunning. The turtle symbolizes slowness, while the fox, deer and rabbit symbolize speed.

In many tribes, competition between two species is common, and the victory is usually the most patient individual and not the fast trusted.

The horse

The Indians believed that the horse was a divine gift. It was called "spiritual dog" or "medical dog" because, according to a Spanish who participated in the expedition of gold-seeker Francisco Vázquez de Coronado in 1541, the natives of the plains used dogs to transport their products. They were used to carry a device known by the French as the travois, which consists of two long poles that are supported in the center to hold the load.

The agricultural villages and the hunters of the plains saw in the horse of the Plains a liberation: a robust, hairy and low-stature horse from a mixture of Andalusian and Arab breeds. It became an indispensable animal for hunters and warriors due to its increased load capacity and mobility.

Women from numerous tribes also had horses, although they were used by warriors and buffalo hunters. The equine and the knight were to be agile not only for bison hunting, but also for inter-tribal fights, such as horse races, which became a characteristic of the life of the plain Indians. Indigenous children and horses were related: they rode on ponies and learned the equestrian skills needed to live as adults. It is essential to have the ability to slide to the galop by the flank of a horse, as this flank acted as a shield on the battlefield.

Hunters and warriors ride on hair or use small, lightweight, filled chairs. The inhabitants of the plains used a heavy wooden chair to mount for less specific purposes. The horses were driven with rings made of uncircumcised trenzed leather and bits made of a piece of the same material. The horse was a powerful tool, symbol of wealth and social status and expression of tribal pride in the plain culture that flourished in the early 19th century. The ability to have a horse was considered prestigious. Some warrior leaders had flocks of more than a thousand animals, and a group of two thousand comanches had up to fifteen thousand cows. When married, the man donated horses to the wife's family, who carried the symbols of the warrior and the tribe to the battlefield. The horse could have helmet prints that represented previous incursions and hand prints representing dead enemies in battle, as well as war emblems that are painted on the sides of aircraft.

Weapons for large animal hunters

In the post-last glacial era, American hunters developed effective weapons to hunt mammots, giant bison and other large, thick-skinned animals that provided them with food and possibly other resources, such as skins. The hunters developed two main types of stone tips, Clovis and Folsom, according to the New Mexico sites in which they were found. They formed a very thin, sharp spear arrow or tip sharpening the center stone to the edges and on both sides. The base of the tip was crocheted to fit firmly into a rod or sleeve.

The whale hunt.

It is a risky activity, as hunters have to penetrate the sea and move in the center of the herd to nail the harpoon on an animal. The effort is worth it because the tons of meat and fat produced by one whale are enough to feed many families.

In the spring, whales migrate north to their summer hives, following the coasts of Alaska and Labrador. Whale hunters travel in an umiak, a drift wooden boat coated with fox leather or morse leather. The length of this type of boat is about nine meters and can accommodate up to ten people. The harpooner claws the weapon when a whale strikes the surface in the vicinity of the boat. The wounded whale quickly submerges and drags a line that is tied to air-filled fox-skin floaters. Each time an animal appears in dispute, the hunters draw more harpoons to it. The whale is exhausted due to wounds and attempts to dive despite the resistance of the floaters, and is eventually sacrificed with a last harponazo.

The hunters untie the dead animal by dragging it to the shore, a difficult manoeuvre because the sea is usually overwhelmed. Residents share meat and fat, while excess meat is stored in "expenditure" excavated in frozen soil. The fat of the whales is melted to produce oil, which is marketed.

Hunting with respect

Arctic and subarctic hunters follow strict standards of respect for their prey. The Mistassini lake cries place food on the fireplace during the feast that they celebrate after the hunt so that the spirits of the dead animals ingest them through the smoke.

Bears are very sensitive and, to frighten the chariots, they place the bones of the broken animal in an elevated tarima. The offender and his family suffer if the bear discovers that their remains have not been treated properly.

Some Inuit believed that the head of the caribou should be cut off once it had been sacrificed to put an end to the sufferings of the Caribou's soul. For the sake of their prey, whale hunters kept the camps clean and organized because they believed they appreciated order.

The Inuit believed that putting ivory amulets depicting the bear and the polar bear on the drag ropes of slaughtered animals attracted favor from the animals and brought luck to the hunter.

The Coyote

It appears in very diverse roles in the central, southwest and western plains of the country. He has different roles, as a creator, trickster, lover and magician. Sometimes, especially in the stories of the tribes of the Great Plains, Coyote appears as the representation of a strong desire and of all potential vices. In many stories, he appears as cruel, deceitful and licentious, seducing his own daughter or grandmother with deceits.

Known for its glutony, the coyote can eat any kind of animal or plant. A preferred motive in the stories is its transformation into a plate, to be able to receive the food that people put in.

He is also depicted as a selfish fool who tries to deceive animals. It almost turns him into a monster because of his lack of pity and ingratitude towards those who help him. In other accounts, however, he is presented as a powerful magician who harmonizes the world and brings significant benefits to humanity. These benefits are often less the result of their own altruism than the indirect result of efforts to satisfy their own selfish appetite.

The Giant and the Coyote

One of the most famous characters in Native American mythology is the coyote. We find him in a variety of roles: creator, cultural hero, trickster, wizard, and lover in the central, southwest and west plains. The character of the coyote, a member of the canine family that stretches from Alaska to Costa Rica, reflects its prominence as spirit and deception. He is quick and clever and can eat any kind of animal or plant. To attract the chariots and devour them, he pretends to be dead. The following Navajo myth perfectly demonstrates the skill of the coyote.

For a long time, giants eager to devour children were spreading across the earth. One day, as he walked through a rocky area, the Coyote stumbled upon one of them and decided to give him a lesson on his cruelty. By promising to make him as agile as he was, he convinced the monster, who was very stupid, to help him build a pavilion for sweat baths. After the dark interior was filled with steam, the Coyote informed him that he would perform a feat: cut off a leg and repair it. He grabbed a stone and struck with force a deer-capped leg that he had hidden in the pavilion, until it broke with a crush. The huge animal touched her broken leg and, deceived, heard the Coyote spit on her and shout, "Oh, leg!" When he touched the Coyote's real leg, the giant was surprised to see it intact. The Coyote offered to do the miracle with the giant's leg, but the monster accepted and shouted in pain when the Coyote struck him with the stone.

She broke up soon and the Coyote told her that I just had to spit on her to fix the problem. The giant spit until his mouth became dry, but the pain remained unbearable for him. In the end, he asked for help. The Coyote advised the child-eater to keep spitting and left the room, leaving the animal in pain.

Coyote is believed to have great creative abilities, according to other myths: In the navel interpretation of the myth about the appearance of tribes, three creative characters are mentioned: the First Man, the First Woman and the Coyote. According to the narrative, after leaving four underground worlds and reaching this one, the Coyote brought seeds from the fourth world and delivered them to the different tribes as they were created.

The Crow

The raven is the animal most frequently mentioned in animal myths. It has a prominent place in North American mythology, as well as in cultures related to Siberia and the Arctic. The horn, and sometimes the spider, is believed to be a sacred being that created the universe and represents age and wisdom.

Killing it is considered illegal in many tribes. The horn is believed to have helped create the earth, animals and humans; it brings light and fresh water; and it teaches people how to live on the earth.

However, it also provokes laughter, makes nonsense and is occasionally lazy. He is cunning, but also a target of deception. Some villages, such as the southern Alaska tlingits, distinguish between two types of crows: the trickster and the cultural hero.

The screaming of birds, especially crows, is the clearest sign of life in the desolate landscape of the far northwest and off the Pacific coast. The raven is distinguished from other species by its black tone, which is explained in the stories by its encounter with a buffalo, gauge or pigeon, in which it is painted black or holly.

The Sacred Pipe

For a long time, Indians have used pipes in their ceremonies. The sacred pipe, in addition to representing the center of the cosmos, is one of the means by which they connect with the past. Remembering this object is like going back to the time when spirits came to the human world and offered them a transcendental gift. The smoke of the pipe carries the prayers of the ancestors.

The Lakotas believe that the sacred pipe came to them through a beautiful spiritual being known as the Thirsty Woman of the White Bison. Two hunters of this tribe saw it, and one of them desired it. A cloud covered it, but when it got up, it left to the surface a great deal of bones. The beautiful woman stood before the tribe and handed over the sacred red pipe, saying, "Observe this pipe!" Always take into account her sacred nature and treat her as such, as this will take you to the end. Don't forget that in me there are four eras. I'm leaving now, but at every moment I'll look back at your town and eventually come back. A member of the Looking Horse family, who resides in the Cheyenne River Reserve in South Dakota, the Bison bull pipe conservationist has been in charge since then.

Share the sacred pipe

One of the oldest and most common rites in the plains and other areas is smoking the sacred pipe. Sharing a pipe reaffirms the connection between family, tribe and the universe, and the pipe itself, often decorated with feathers and drawings, represents creation.

The origins of the sacred pipe of the Lakotas are explained in the following myth. It is believed that the pipe still exists, unlike the sacred stone, and very few people have seen it.

Many winters ago, a beautiful and mysterious woman, dressed in white front and with a burden on her back, approached two lame hunters. One of the men expressed his desire for her and immediately fell into ruins. The woman expressed her desire to talk to her leader. Go see him and ask him to make a big coat. The hunter obeyed the order.

On arriving at the tipi, the woman handed over the bag to the leader and expressed: "I am the woman White Buffalo". No unclean man should contemplate this, for it is sacred. In the coming winters, this action will allow you to transmit your voice to Wakan Tanka. He took a pipe and a small round stone out of the bag and put them on the floor. Then, raising the pipe with the cannon toward the sky, he expressed: "With this sacred pipe you will walk on the earth, for the earth is your grandmother and mother and is sacred." The red stone on the pipe pot represents the earth. A young buffalo engraved on the stone represents all four-legged beings. Everything that grows is represented in the wooden cannon. The Moteed Eagle has twelve feathers that hang on the pipe and symbolize all beings in the air. The pipe will be used in the seven rites in which the seven circles of the stone are used.

After talking about the first rite, the woman White Buffalo announced her departure and said she would come back someday. Before the other rites were revealed, the woman announced her return. It turned into an adult black buffalo, then into a young red and brown buffer. He lifted up his head toward the whole cosmos and disappeared in the middle of the mountain.

The rituals of the Lakota pipe

In the round stone left by the woman White Buffalo, seven circles were engraved, representing the seven rites related to the pipe, according to the Lakota myth.

The first ritual, the maintenance and release of the soul, aims to "keep" the soul of a deceased for several years, until it is adequately released and ensures its return to the spirit world. The second rite is the sweat pavilion, which is a purification rite preceding all the others.

The third, the cry for the vision, traces the ritual model of the search for vision, when a person throws himself in solitary search for a sacred vision. The fourth is a community recreation ceremony known as the dance of the sun. The fifth is family formation, a ritual union of two friends with a sacred bond. The sixth is the female puberty ceremony and the last is "throwing the ball"

Ritual dances

The dance of the sun

The sun dance, the most important ritual in the region, reflects the role of the sun as a creative force and source of power in the mythology of the plains, which is preserved, modified, among some peoples.

The tribe meets once a year, usually at the beginning of the summer, to honor their beliefs with a series of ceremonies, songs, and other rites. The center of the celebration is the dance of the sun, a ritual performed by those seeking to obtain spiritual power in front of the tribe, which forms a wide circle around a pole, a symbolic bond between the higher and lower worlds.

The dancers move around the pole, sometimes for whole days, until they finally disappear into a frenetic state or complete exhaustion. Some dancers inflicted wounds on themselves, as tearing the flesh represents liberation from the constraints of ignorance.

The Survival of the Sun Dance

White observers were scandalized by self-flagellation in the 19th century, so it was banned in 1881. This was a hard blow for the Plain Indians because they believed that the dance of the sun would be ineffective without this essential element and the world would not be renewed. Many Indians throughout the following years devoted themselves to performing public sun dances for the entertainment of the whites and simulated drilling meat with harnesses.

Others celebrated it in secret, such as the traditional drilling. Guards were placed at a certain distance to warn of the arrival of white officers.

Although the Indian Reorganization Act of 1934 allowed for drilling again, the full renaissance occurred in the 1960s due to the rise of Indian militance. Today, sun dance is practiced in most of the indigenous reserves of the plains and in some urban areas.

The Cheyene Sun Dance is a creation of Indian artist Dick West. The dancer hangs from the leather strips that hold him from the chest in the sun dance shelter. The tension of the leather strips increases with the bison skulls subjected to their back.

The Dance of Spirits

The Dance of the Spirits, which originated among the paiutes, was the most popular and widespread of all the millennial movements. The movement never formed as a single movement, but rather as a collection of very similar revitalization cults derived from the same source. A common feature of all of them is a circular dance in which the dancers, in a state of sleep, contemplate their deceased loved ones.

More than a tenth of the Paiute population died of diseases in 1870. In the Fish Lake Valley, in the present Utah state, a wovoka, also known as the "time doctor", dreamed that he had the ability to bring back the souls of the recently deceased, thanks to his alleged ability to control rain, earthquakes, and other natural phenomena. According to his dream, to it, it was necessary to paint and perform circular dances. This wovoka became Wodziwob, a paiute word for an old man, a healer or a doctor. During the dancers' rest, Wodziwob arrived at a time when he assured to visit the deceased, who assure him that he would soon return with his loved ones. Wodziwob's fame spread to California, the Great Basin and the Plateau, mainly thanks to the work of another physician of the time, Tavibo. However, Wodziwob declared in 1872 that he had been deceived by an evil witch-buh, which prompted a rapid end to the Dance of the Paiute Spirits.

Tavibo's son, who had also received medical training at the time, reintroduced the Dances of the Spirits and became Wovoka.

Wovoka learned Christianity, worked at a Mormon ranch and was named Jack Wilson in English. During his illness on January 1, 1889, Wovoka had a moment in which he claimed to have visited the land of the dead, where God had asked him to preach peace. According to

Wovoka, the natives could see the deceased during the circular dances and visit the ancient world of the traditional Indians. He urged the Indians not to fight and even asked them to adopt white customs to promote peace.

Many rural communities sent envoys to Wovoka. Each community adjusted its message to meet its own needs. The Lakota version had Christian influences and was more revolutionary than its model. The Lakots believed that Wovoka was the son of the Great Spirit, who had risen from the dead after being murdered by the white. A cloud of fire would wipe out the whites over time, the dead and the bison would return and start a new world. Many Lakotas, as elsewhere, wore special Dancing of the Spirits shirts, thinking they protected them from bullets.

The U.S. Army used the spread of the Dance of the Spirits as an excuse to disarm all indigenous communities in the meadows. During one of these operations in Wounded Knee, South Dakota, in December 1890, troops killed 200 Lakotas. Wounded Knee is for Indians a reminder of how the whites ended the Dance of the Spirits and native culture in general.

The religious and healing dance of the Chippewa

For the Chippewa, summer was the season of village life. In the spring, when people gathered in the villages for the Midewiwin, or Healing Dance, it was celebrated again in the fall, before the groups separated due to winter hunting.

The most important collective religious ritual of the Chippewa, the Midewiwin, included many ancient elements, especially the origin myth about Wenebojo, a cunning cultural hero, a part of which was told during the ceremony. The dance was exclusively for the initiated members. The application for participation in Midewiwin could be motivated by illness or even the death of a close family member; or it could be Motivated by a dream indicating the duty to join that group. A person could reach different levels of initiation by repeating that dance several times.

Although Midewiwin rituals vary by community, the typical representation consisted of a parade around the cabin-medicine in the opposite direction of the clock, accompanied by drums and chants. The ceremony reached its peak when some selected members of the group "shoot" the new initiate magic, directing his healing skins and supposedly injecting small white shells into his body.

Dance Contest

The championships are organized in groups according to the type of dance, age and gender, and usually include traditional, fantasy, grass, mantle and cascade dances. Participants wear suitable clothes for the type of dance they perform.

A fantasy artist adorns her body with feathers and cushions, while a dancer with mantles wears a chalice of long flecos on her dress, mocassins and polenas carefully adorned with counts. This name is given to the performers of the dance with cascades due to the bells that decorate their costumes.

The judges, who are often powwows competition champions, judge the contestants and not only their mastery of style, but also their ability to follow the rhythm of the song and finish the dance with the last touch of the drum. The winners usually make one for the audience to applaud them.

The Dancers of the Serpents

The ceremonies to invoke rain are one of the most important events of the annual rituals in the arid lands of the southwest. The most important are performed by specialized sacred groups, such as the hopis snake dancers, whose one-week rites are held every two years at the end of the summer. The hopis believe that the snake's sinuous shape resembles the lightning that precedes the rain. They want the dances to be a great demonstration of community respect for the offices that produce the rain that allows crops.

During the first four days of the ceremony, members of the society are interned in the desert to catch snakes and take them to the village. The members of the holy societies of the hopis ritually represent the primordial events during the next two days and two nights in a ceremonial chamber or chamber. During the rest of the celebration, races, dances (priests holding with their mouths mortal snakes, even cascabel) and the final blessing are held. The offices are collected and sent back to the desert. By the late 19th century, photographs of snake dances became so popular among white Americans that there was an army of photographers who competed with each other and altered sacred rituals. The hopis gradually established a ban on visitors taking photographs during the ceremonies, which remains in force today.

The renaissance of spiritual dance.

In 1973, members of the Indian American Movement occupied

Wounded Knee for several weeks. The spiritual leader of the occupation, Leonard Crow Dog, always believed that the Lakotas emissaries who spoke to Wovoka had misinterpreted his message.

When they should have seen circular dance as a means of keeping traditions alive, creating a link with history and ancestors, they believed that they could bring back the dead.

Crow Dog directed a Dance of the Spirits at the site of the 1890 massacre during the protest. Thro the night, the women worked making shirts for the dance with curtains and arpillers painted in the traditional style.

Many of the dancers wore reversed American flags, which is a common way of expressing their dissatisfaction with the Movement.

Crow Dog has practised the Dancing of Spirits at Crow dog's Paradise, a family-owned property in the Rosebud Reserve in South Dakota, since 1973.

Social organization

The stereotyped image of North American Indians is full of Eurocentric ideas about the family and how communities are organized. Many times it was the same missionaries and government officials who conveyed these ideas to the Indians. The Indian family was nuclear and patriarchal, with the husband as the leader and monogamous couples living in the same house. It seemed that the social organization was basically democratic, but it was led by a leader who oversaw internal affairs and acted as a link between the tribe and others.

However, this type of social organization was not common. In general, families were not nuclear, but rather "united", that is, several generations shared a home. Not all marriages were monogamous: in many Indian communities, a person could have multiple spouses, provided that the family could be sustained financially. Clan relations were as important as individual family relations, and often formed the basis of political structures. The government of the communities had various forms, from the assembly to the "dictature" of a powerful leader or king, such as the "king of the sun" of the southeastern natchez, who inherited the title.

The hunting and harvesting communities were patriarchal and patrilineal, which meant that men controlled almost all possessions and made decisions, and inheritance followed the male line. Several of this general pattern were practised in many prairie, Arctic, Subarctic, Plateau, and California communities. A man, his wives and his children formed the typical family unit of fifteen to twenty-five people. It could include the families of the male children as well. The size of the family unit generally depended on the land. The daughters who married left the family. During times of abundance, these small groups united with others to form larger units to celebrate rituals, arrange marriages, and organize hunting, war, incursions, territorial disputes, and other matters.

He used to rely on personal merits, such as hunting or war skills, to lead. A chief could only remain in his position as long as the community considered his skills and experience necessary.

On the other hand, agricultural communities were typically matriarchal and matrilineal, where women were in charge of managing land possessions and land use. Some prairie farming communities, such as the mandanes, and many eastern forest nations, fit into this general pattern. Families were large and "united", consisting of a woman, her husband or husbands, her daughters and the families of her daughter, all living in a dwelling, which could be a long house or a cabin of adobe. Mother-to-daughter ownership of arable land, political power and some sacred activities were passed on. Sometimes, clans (family groups) were subdivided into halves, which were led by men who had descent from certain groups of women. Halves were in charge of the sacred hatches and planned plans for war or peace for the entire community. Personal merits were valued, but leadership was based more on inheritance or title. For collective action, consensus was required, but heads had the power to take decisions on behalf of the group. Complex family structures collaborated with societies that transcended family ties to carry out certain ritual or secular activities.

Some communities were distinguished by the importance they attached to the social position, to the point that there was some sort of division into social classes. In some situations, the position was based on wealth, while in others, material possessions were less important, and prestige based on personal qualities such as generosity, which was always highly appreciated because it contributed to the survival of the group. Clans and social groups acted as mutual aid organizations through exchanges, gifts and costly ceremonies such as potlatch, ensuring that no one lacked the essential to survive.

Maintaining Traditions
The fundamental beliefs of the Indians have remained solid despi-

te the numerous changes they have experienced since the arrival of the first white settlers. Essentially, these beliefs maintain that a Creator established the natural laws and sacred rites, which are immutable. Recently, Viola Hatch, a Southern Cheyen woman, explained that we do not have written rules that dictate how we should live. The Great Spirit has given it to us. He said it to us once, we learned it and we have done it so far. The Indians believe that the sacred past will always be at hand, and that nature's sacred cycles will continue as always, even though the material circumstances of a people may change. My people, my family and my sacred relations with animals, plants and spirits are the most essential elements of native life that no catastrophe or human intervention can alter. Matthew King, an elder of the Lakota tribe, expresses it in this way: "We have been here for millions of years. God gave us laws that allowed us to organize our society. There's no way to change them. No one has the ability to modify them. We can't make laws.

Maintaining the traditional customs of Native Americans has been based on oral tradition. Each generation learns history, traditional morality and how ancient rituals and ceremonies were carried out. This maintenance of oral tradition is crucial because it prevents ancient stories from being anchored, a trend that occurs when sacred stories are written. The details of each story change to reflect new situations in people's lives.

Sacred objects, such as those stored in sacred hatches, also help to maintain traditional traditions. Hats may contain objects that allegedly belonged to the early ancestors of a clan, making them a complete document of their history. The personal sacred hatches, which are revealed in visions or dreams, remind their owner of their personal relationship with the spirit world. If a cock sees a castor in a dream, make a hole with castor skin and add stones, counts and parts of animals that he believes will give him spiritual power.

The contents of a sacred hat can be updated periodically, in the same way that the details of ancient tales transmitted by oral tradition are updated. Each time the owner receives new spiritual revelations, he adds or removes elements from his hole. This willingness to change is the main factor that has enabled the natives to remain in force in the modern world.

The power of women

The woman was the microcosm of Mother Earth in giving life. The Indians venerated women for this reason and sometimes feared their powers. They regarded the first menstruation as a period of extraordinary power and potential dangers, similar to other times of transition, in which the body was in a state of physical and spiritual instability.

The young woman used to be isolated in a small hut apart from the village as part of the transitional rituals that mark the first menstruation. He was explained to several taboos that he had to comply with during his subsequent menstruation, including the belief that menstrual blood was a highly dangerous substance and that if mixed with sacred objects it could take away its power and cause disease. For many women, it was a great challenge, as every month they spent several days unable to perform their daily tasks. Moreover, it was a period of recovery and rest.

The Lakotas referred to the periods of isolation during the Isanti menstruation as "living in solitude". Menstruation was believed to be a natural purification, so women did not need to undergo the traditional ritual cleansing in the sweat shelter, as men did.

The first Kinaalda is carried out to honor the menstruation of the figure called the Changing Woman, who is the daughter of the First Man with the First Woman and the ancestor of the Navajo, four days after birth. Even today, the Kinaalda is used as part of the "path of blessings", a cycle of ceremonies that includes all the Navajo transition rites.

Women growing corn

Women play an important role in many sacred corn ceremonies, and the creation of this cereal is usually associated with a female figure. According to the Cherokee belief, the first woman, known as Selu ("Maize"), gave birth to the first plant after rubbing her belly. At the green corn ceremony, Selu, who also created the first green Jewish women from her breasts, is honoured by young people carrying baskets with the first plants harvested of the year.

The Zuñis and other Southwest Indian peoples believe that the Six Maize Wives were the first people to grow corn. Two kachinas sisters (spirits) called the Blue Corn Girl and the Yellow Corn Girl participate in rituals commemorating the return of the sun during the hopis' New Year celebrations, which take place during the winter solstice season.

According to the orders, Túnica de Buena Piel founded the Cow Society, a group of women who were responsible for different aspects of the planting, care and harvest of corn, as well as various rituals related to the corn ritual. The cows generally had an average age of thirty years, but could incorporate into society much earlier. The maize priest oversaw their activities and gradually increased their rank.

During the corn growing season, the Cow Society performed dances that were related to the migration of these birds that represented the grain and considered messengers of the Old Man Who Never Dies, who was responsible for their growth.

Powwow

It is likely that this word comes from the algonquino term pauau, which means gathering people. Americans of European descent use it without exception to refer to any social meeting or event where important topics are discussed.

However, for the Indians, powwow refers to a numerous and traditional, secular, tribal or intertribal encounter, which includes singing, dancing, gift-sharing and tribute ceremonies. They are excellent public manifestations of Indian identity. Although they are sometimes accessible to the entire population, most of the time they focus on the natives themselves. Inter-tribal powwows are obviously more numerous than tribal ones, but regardless of their size, they are an important means of transmission of Indian traditions.

Indians travel a powwow path or circuit through the territory from late spring to early autumn with the aim of participating in powwows within tribes. Pan-Indian encounters enable tribal members to establish relationships with other Aboriginal groups, making them a demonstration of solidarity among Native Americans and a profound expression of Indian culture.

The powwow, which normally takes place in a central or "emparated" space, begins with an entry from the top. Military veterans generally lead the opening parade, carrying out the flag ceremony and pronouncing a brief invocation. War dances and other types, such as round, grass and rabbit dances, often follow them. Many of these dances have a very specific internal tribal purpose. The Powwow dancers slide with great elegance and the constant sound of the drum directs their movements. They are embellished with mantles, clothes decorated with counts, polysons and touched complexes. Dance competitions are one of the many powwows. Since dancers and drummers receive significant amounts of money, contestants often travel long distances to participate.

The gift-sharing ceremony is another significant moment in the powwow, in which a person or family delivers gifts to another person, which can be as complex as hand-made "star" edredons by the sioux or as simple as kitchen utensils. This ceremony serves as a way of honouring those members of the community who have been distinguished for some reason, such as university graduates, members of military personnel and community leaders. In addition, they often honor those who have helped a family in difficult times, such as during the mourning. Between a dance and another, the gifts are distributed during the afternoon. Ceremonial master Powwow explains the motives for the gift, as well as the identity of donors and recipients, and proposes an honorary dance. The dance program continues after the participants give each other a hand.

Social exchanges are as important as dances in Powwow. They help Indians from different tribes renew old friendships and share a banquet serving traditional indigenous foods such as bison, veal, cornweed and fried bread. Indians often make political prayers and speeches, and occasionally take the opportunity to earn more money by selling handicrafts.

The shaking tent

The Ogibwas are aware that human help is not always enough and that at times, the people need to resort to sacred beings to solve their problems. They have created various ways of interacting with these beings or "grandparents", who are considered to be very present in the ojibwa culture.

One of the ways to get in direct contact with grandparents is to visit the refuge of adivining, also known as the "trembling tent". The store itself is a barrel-shaped post structure, which has a height of two meters. It is put outdoors and covered with canvas, leather or beetroot bark.

Activities such as guessing or hand games are carried out in the interior with the aim of identifying the causes of a disease or finding a lost object. The prestidigitator enters the tabernacle at night and calls the beings who are his pawaganak or guardian spirits.

He can invoke the souls of living beings (not human beings) and of the dead, whose arrival is evident when the spirits embodying the winds shake the tent. Sometimes, the prestigitator is tied with ropes and there are no human acts at stake.

Spiritual voices often mention their own names or sing; they may be animals or well-known mythological characters.

In some cases, the present may speak directly to the beings and ask them to answer their questions at that time.

Warrior Strikes

During their career as warriors, the Dakota men increased their military rank through different "coupes": actions that demonstrated their courage in battle.

Each category allowed the warrior to wear different feathers, which could be cut, cut or dyed according to the type of blow. These are some examples.

1. The red-tinted pen symbolizes the wound suffered on the battlefield.

2. The red pen indicates the death of an opponent.

3. A pen with a punch ripped off the scalp and cut off the neck of an enemy.

4. An enemy cut off his neck with a pen with the tip cut off.

5. He struck four times with a pen with the edge closed.

6. The pen was partially furry and gave five beats.

The drum has the shape of a circle.

The rounding of the drum in Native American philosophy represents the inseparable unity of the past, present and future. All people are connected in this unit like a circle. The rhythm of the drum is a representation of the unbreakable rhythms of nature. These rhythms can be seen in the stories of modern Indian writers and in the way the traditional narrator speaks.

A beat of the drum

For Indian dancers, the drum rhythm represents the human pulse and the fundamental rhythms of life. For this reason, dances have always played an important role in native expression, and in recent years, both dance and music have experienced an extraordinary resurgence. Non-traditional visual forms, such as theatre and fine arts, have also been a form of expression of Indian creativity. Although Pan-Indian themes are sometimes also addressed, the artistic manifestations of the Indians are often related to the traditions and interests of specific tribes. Many songs and dances are inter-tribal and are included in the repertoire of such prestigious companies as the American Indian Dance Theater.Native musicians such as R. Carlos Nakai and Kevin Locke have received international praise for their flute performances, compositions and dances. Many Indian artists have managed to stand out on the "New Age" circuit, however, others prefer more conventional styles. For example, sioux-yankton children between the ages of seven and fourteen, called Ihankton-wan Singers, usually perform in the northern region of the plains.

Native theatre is also flourishing, especially in Canada, where the leading Canadian Aboriginal theatre company, Native Earth Performing Arts, represents works by important Indian authors such as Joyce B. Joe and Thomson Highway.

The Northern Plains Tribal Arts Exhibition in Sioux Falls, South Dakota in September brings together artists from all over the region and attracts thousands of spectators. Artworks such as paintings and sculptures on indigenous themes are exhibited there, using a wide variety of abstract and figurative styles. In addition, works are performed in conventional forms, as well as music and dances: there are artists who perform ancient Indian melodies, as are groups of country and western music and protest song. The great interest aroused by the resurrection of native art is reflected in the success of this exhibition and the opening of Native galleries throughout North America.

Rituals for Transition

Many native North American cultures mark the crucial moments of each person's life, such as birth, puberty, adolescence, marriage and death, with meaningful rituals that symbolize the transition from the pre-state to the new one. They believe that, in those moments of physical transition, the person in question is very close to the spiritual world, which turns him into a state full of potential and risks.

Newborns and newborns are extremely fragile, and many tribes ha-veined the tradition of following taboos to protect children from the greatest possible harm. A cherokee who was pregnant avoided tasting the strawberries for fear that her offspring would be born with stains on her face. Eggs were rejected by the Apaches because they believed that they caused blindness and that the animal's tongue caused the child to delay in learning to speak.

Most civilizations have rites that accompany the transition from childhood to adulthood. Its structure is very similar to that of most indigenous cultures and tribal societies around the world. They usually include a period of physical isolation, which marks the moment the person breaks ties with his previous condition. This brief social exile serves as an intermediate state of "not being" and usually consists of a test of physical resistance, pain or deprivation. The incorporation into the new life condition is usually completed by a ritual. Almost all of these elements were present in the Nozihzho rite of the Omahas, which means "sleeping standing." The ritual consisted of a four-day fast followed by all Omaha teenage males and any girl who desired it. The name refers to the mood that young people experience during the ceremony. They kept themselves away from their surroundings and only had knowledge of their own inner identity. The Omaha myth of the origins was recreated in this ritual. To honour the animals who reached the bottom of a large mass of water and returned with the mud from which the earth was created, the teenager sought an isolated place and sprinkled his head with clay. He prayed to Wakoda, the mysterious power that ruled nature. The teenager thought of health, good hunting, successes in the war and a happy and happy life, but it was illegal to ask for special favors.

The Omahas believed that Wakoda responded with a sacred song in a vision or dream. Dreaming of hawks, alms or thorns could be a sign of good luck. The song was a lucky amulet that connected the teenager with the powers of the universe and could use it throughout his life to ask for help from the guardian spirits in difficult times.

After performing the ritual, the teenager took a four-day break and listened to the words of an old man who had had had a similar dream. Then he searched and killed the animal he had seen in his dreams, and kept a fragment as a sacred possession in his personal medicinal hole. This object was taken to the battlefield or used in rituals.

The Nozhizho ritual contained risks. The idea of dreaming of snakes generated difficulties. The teenager had to abandon the idea of becoming a man and adopt the customs of a woman, living like a little bitch receiving instructions from the moon, if he dreamed of the Moon and woke up at the wrong time. He dressed himself like women, and wore long hair instead of shaving his head, except for the strap that went from neck to forehead, as men did, because of his condition of mixuga. Instead of hunting and warfare, she devoted herself to agriculture, planting, harvesting and the practice of female arts.

The courtship required very special customs. The Lakotas offered a serenade to the young women and played a special flute for the courtship, which often included animal scales, especially of birds such as ducks, grullas and prairie faisanes, known for their spectacular "dances" of courtesy. They believed that the flute, often made by sacred beings, had powerful magic notes that allowed the woman to travel everywhere with her beloved.

Aboriginal Americans used to see marriage as a state that persisted until death, which can be observed in the wedding rites of some communities. The hopis used to marry at dawn. Towards the rising sun, the couple spread corn flour across the eastern edge of the table. The groom's family woven two white cotton wedding tunics with blades and blades for the bride. The bride only wore one during the wedding because the other was destined to be her mortuary. Therefore, uniform clothing confirmed the woman's married status and, at the time of her death, facilitated her entry into the spirit world.

Illustrations and symbols

To express their relationship with the sacred land and the plants and animals with whom they share it, peoples of all native American cultures resort to artistic manifestations. The symbols and drawings that adorn from the squirrels to the shoes allow artists and peoples to reflect on the world around them and remember their religious and secular importance. Objects carefully crafted should be appreciated by their own users and, traditionally, artistic skill is highly appreciated. For Indian peoples, as in other cultures, having access to the best artists and craftsmen was an unambiguous indicator of social prestige.

Decorative drawings and symbols can be used in almost any type of material or applied to other objects. The skins are adorned with counts or feathers and painted. The horn, bone, shell, stone and wood are cut, engraved and painted. Clay figures or squirrels are also often painted or engraved. Animal hair and plant fibers are filed to make nets and tissues.

The medium limits the subjects to some extent. Because they are the easiest fabrics to work, cisterns, counts and woven fabrics generally have geometric drawings. The naturalist figures experience some stylization due to the limitations of the material. Although loyalty to nature is not necessarily an artistic or cultural ideal, painting and sculptures tend to present a greater naturalism.

Most of the time, the symbols and drawings reflect the natural environment of the artist. For example, floral and vegetable motifs are used in forest art, while marine animals are more common in coastal groups.

Other themes are based on the cosmology of the respective peoples and often appear mythical beings such as the thunderbird, snakes and other supernatural creatures.

Several territories, including the southwest and northwest coast, are known for their basket experts. Both the ceremonial and daily baskets of the hopis usually carry geometric drawings, animals and kachinas. The most common themes are triangles and concentric circles, which often include vibrant colors and elaborate designs. Although eagle and fox mother kachina are popular themes, turtles have gained popularity recently.

The Alfareros villages are recognized for their high quality and sophistication in their works, which maintain the tradition rooted in the large pre-contact cultures of the area, such as the Anasazis.

Both geometric themes and traditional animals, such as snakes and thunderbirds, are represented in white, black and in intense red, ocres and natural creams.

More than thirty thousand Navajo indigenous people are engaged in the weaving of carpets, resulting in great diversity. According to the Navajo legend, the Spider Woman taught the weavers how to grind herbs, yuca, cedar bark and cotton. However, wool became the main raw material for the navajos as they engaged in pasturing. In order to adapt to the tourist market, Navajo carpets have adopted pastel tones instead of natural terrestrial tones. There are a variety of local modalities. The glass style, for example, uses a lot of different lines. The Yei carpets (which means "god") and Yeibichai (who means "masked dancer") are inspired by the sacred paintings on sand, although they do not have a ritual function. In the Great Lakes area, skilled employees flatten pork-spin threads, adorn them with vegetable dyes and use them to decorate bags and mocassins. The women of the northeastern tribes Huron, Micmac and others embroidered leather, fabrics, and bark of beetle with hair dyed with bark. As the Europeans introduced colored glass counts in the region, the Indians combined them with traditional materials and even replaced them. Although complex floral themes are the most common, they also use simple geometric drawings to decorate objects such as bags or knife vines.

The villages of the plains also used pig-spin puffs for mocassins and pipes. The drawings of the Indians of the plains are usually more geometric and include circles, rectangles and triangles, but bison skins covering the tipis and those of particular use may present naturalistic images of buffaloes and horses. The circles represent the celestial dome, the buffalo land shelter or the soil of the tipi. The circle, as in many other native cultures of North America, represents the relationship between what exists on earth and the eternal cycles of nature.

Much of the art of the northwest coast is considered figurative, i.e. it highlights the elements or characteristics of an animal or person and, at times, removes other traits. The castor is represented by two large incisives and a wide, shaded tail, while the horns have a peak and eyes that give them a unique appearance. The representation of the three-dimensional totemic poses is usually more complete than in two dimensional objects. Although some animal figures combine animal and human traits, they often adopt anthropomorphic characteristics.

Masks

The actors wore masks that represented different supernatural beings with healing powers in many ceremonies, especially those intended to heal the sick. The Yei masks of the Navajo are made of ceremonial gamuzas of sacrificed deer. To prevent blood loss, the deer should be stifled using sacred flour or corn pollen in the nasal holes.

Masks are used in the winter healing ritual Yeibichai, also known as the Night Song. This ritual can only be performed during the night, when the snakes are asleep. The ceremony is held in order to heal people affected by attacks or madness.

However, during the final two nights of the ceremony, the Yeibichais teach young men of both sexes the secrets of the masquerading gods.

Ceremonial suits and costumes

The mythical custom or religious vision dictated the ceremonial costumes worn by members of the tribe, especially chiefs and warriors. While the feathers used to be eagles, the skin and horns of the buffalo were used to make feather or other touches.

The shape of the models, the decorated shirts and the drawings painted on men and horses had a mythical meaning. They wore this type of suit on ceremonial occasions, such as returning from a successful incursion or in the same battles.

The tribes used the decorative materials at their natural reach. Thus, the cree of the plains were skilled in making ornaments with dyed spinach pig legs, while the blackfoot wore cornea and buho feathers. It was believed that in any case, the special qualities of animals were passed on to the user.

Family and spirit

For many Indian peoples, kinship was essential to the stability, integrity and survival of the community. For example, being a nephew or daughter means playing a specific role with clearly defined rights and obligations in relation to others. Foreigners arriving in the villages, including white prisoners, were often regarded as "cousins" or "brothers", which guaranteed their stable social position and the integrity of the group.

The elders played a very significant role. By tradition, grandparents were responsible for almost all of their children's upbringing because parents were believed to be too busy with daily tasks and had not yet attained the wisdom to pass it on to their children. The elders were and remain the source of food and moral formation, as well as the recipient of the mythological and spiritual heritage of each people, as narrators. First of all, they are responsible forining the sacred customs of the community.

Indians often see the community as an extension of the natural world, with abundant spirits. Clans (or families) and sacred communities were believed to be descendants of an animal or totem, a term that anthropologists have adopted from the ojibwa odem language, which translates as "village". For example, the Iroquois are organized into clans called "turtle clan", "bear clan" and "wolf clan," with a mother clan leading each.

The totemic animal may have helped an ancestor hunt or find the way home. In other situations, a member of the clan is looking for an animal to turn it into the totem of his group.

According to members of the Osage spider clan, on one occasion, a child participated in an expedition to the forest in search of a totemic animal. He found the fabric of a large spider as he followed the footprints of a deer. She questioned the reason for her clash with the spider. The young man replied that he was following the footsteps of a deer because he was looking for a strong animal to turn it into a symbol of his clan. The spider claimed that, although it looked like a tiny and weak creature, it had the exceptional virtue of patience.

Moreover, sooner or later they were all captured by them, as happened to man. The boy was impressed by that explanation and returned to his clan, where he adopted the spider as a totem animal.

Individuals who were not part of a totem-based society or clan were able to develop a personal relationship with a Totem animal, which became their spiritual guide. It was often believed that clans and people adopted the characteristics of the spiritual totem. It was said, for example, that the members of the bear clan were extremely strong and fierce. The mice are very short-sighted, and the mice-clan cheyenes adopted a short world view: they paid much attention to the near and present things and little or nothing to the long or future things.

The Red Road

In the vision of Black Alce, Grandpa describes the concept of the Red Way, which extends from where the giant resides (the north) to where you always look (el sur). Your nation must follow the path of good and follow it. It is a sacred path that connects the past and the future, a path that everyone can travel.

The Red Way can be defined as a way of addressing the current problems of Indians using native traditional values such as courage, spirituality and respect for the family. The Red Way contributes to strengthening Indian identity in the dominant society. First of all, it is the way that Native Americans control their own destiny.

Many Indians use the Red Way approach to address contemporary social problems such as alcoholism and drug addiction, which in some cases affect many families. For example, alcoholism is one of the main factors contributing to domestic violence and increased suicide rates among native youth. Various programmes called the Red Way have been created to address these problems. The Gene Alce Delgado Program in eastern South Dakota prepares monitors for the rehabilitation of alcoholics and drug addicts through retreats, classes and traditional ceremonies. The results have been remarkable: in the communities that have opted for this programme, Alce Delgado's proposal has been more successful than Alcoholics Anonymous.

The Red Road approach has also been applied to the problem of unemployment in India, which in some communities exceeds 85%. Despite the gravity of the situation, local plans for economic growth based on the classic values of commitment and generosity are yielding good results. In the 1980s, Wilma P. Mankiller, the Chief Supreme Chief of the Cherokee country, and her husband, Charlie Soap, created a small business advisory and credit system to help and cooperatives in areas with high unemployment and low wages.

The resurgence of native values has also affected tribal government. The Indian Reorganization Act of 1934 imposed on tribes Euro-American rules of representative government, mainly in the form of elected tribal councils. However, representative democracy violated numerous traditions of assembly government, in which all members of the tribe had direct consultation on important decisions. Currently, some Indian nations have tried to regain more traditional forms of tribal government, which work parallel to the official system, although all tribes must maintain their tribal councils to deal with the Office of Indian Affairs and other federal or state agencies. For example, the ihanktonwan tribe (sioux yankton) has restored a consensual system in which the 7,000 census members of the tribe can intervene directly in the tribal council to influence the drafting of laws and regulations, from the awarding of casino gains and the curricula of the new community university to the preservation of traditional culture.

The Red Way can also facilitate often conflicting relationships between natives and non-natives. Some Indians, such as the Lakota Wallace Black Swan (a sacred man who, although he has no blood kinship with the famous black swan, considers himself his spiritual kinsman), strive to spread the Red Way among the whites. Not all Indians agree with the idea of revealing to strangers the traditions and sacred practice. The Red Way has been used as a basis for inter-ethnic reconciliation programmes in South Dakota and Minnesota, where Indian-White relations have often been unstable.

The success of the Red Way initiatives demonstrates that traditional Indian methods remain dynamic and can be applied to current problems. For many Indians, the Red Way is crucial toining a native lifestyle in the twenty-first century.

Medicinal plants

Traditional Indian healers use a wide range of medicinal plants, and many of the findings they made were used in Western medicine. For example, the remedy for squirrels made from oak bark or sauce contains salicin, an active ingredient of aspirin.

Doctors use Hamamelis virginiana, a plant known as the "witch plant", to treat muscle pain.

Since 1878, the best-selling laxative in the U.S. has been made from the bark of another bush called Phammus purshiana. Salvia was one of the aromatic plants used in ritual fumigations, in which participants were "bathed" in smoke or inhaled to purify themselves. Sage infusions are also used to treat numerous diseases. Salvia columbariae is a species of salvia that Numlakis in California use extensively.

Rituals involving plants

Plants were venerated as gifts from Mother Earth and provided more food than hunting for almost all Aboriginal peoples. Some Indian nations had special relationships with specific plants, such as corn, on which they depended for their livelihoods and whose survival depended on human cultivators.

The earliest domesticated plants, such as sunflower, peach and amarant, were grown in temperate areas, on the banks of rivers and in villages, where the removed soil rich in hydrogen was ideal for its production. Maize, the most important domesticated plant in Central America, was first grown in central America around 6000 B.C. and since 1000 it was produced in latitudes as northern as southern Canada, wherever the number of ice-free days and the level of precipitation allowed. In the prehistoric city of Cahokia, it fed thirty thousand people, and had a significant impact on the worldview and ceremonial life of almost every group for which it constituted the main harvest. For example, in the Arikara myths of the origins, the figure of Mother Maize was very important. Both the Mandanes and the Pawnees of the plains and the Choctaw of the southeast valued corn.

The washos' lifestyle, for example, was based on the collection of plants. They were forced to store seeds, roots, and dried fruit to survive the winter in one of the coldest regions of western North America. Families were constantly travelling to get the necessary quantity of abundant but scattered plants. Washos were very relevant at the time of harvest because the skills to find and process specific plants were transmitted from mother to daughter. Most of the seeds had to be peeled, broken and grated to turn them into flour, while some dried fruits, such as bellotas, needed to be licked to extract the toxic components. The need to collect food forced the washos to live in scattered groups for most of the year. They gathered in the autumn to collect pineapples, a term used to refer to all pines that produce edible fruit. Collecting the fruits of pineapples or gumsaba was a time of great rituals and social activities, as the pines produced a wealth that surpassed that of other plants.

Numerous wild plants were used in rituals and healing therapies by Native Americans. For ritual purification, they used salvia and bathed themselves with the smoke of this plant. They widely utilized the healing properties of a variety of plants. To alleviate indigestion, they prepared infusions with leaves of various plants and chewed certain roots to calm the throat and headache. Tobacco was widely used in ritual practices, whether cultivated or wild.

Medical wheels

In the plains and meadows of North America you can find large circles of stone known as "medical wheels". They were constructed using the small rolled corners that left the glaciers on the surface of the earth. Each wheel has its center formed by a pile or a large number of stones, and there are often others around the circumference. Sometimes, stone lines range from the central pile to the outer circle in the form of radii.

The medical wheel of Big Horn in Wyoming is the most famous of these structures. It measures approximately 30 meters in diameter, has 28 radii and has an outer circle with six small piles of stones. We don't know who the builders were, when it was built and why. According to the most widely accepted hypothesis, the "rays" of the medicinal wheel are related (or at least were at the beginning) to astronomical events.

According to another hypothesis, they can play a symbolic role and be visual representations of the cyclical sacred principles that unite the universe. They resemble the forms found in the dances and in the structure of some Aboriginal shelters. Many of them are found in high terrain and may represent the celestial vault.

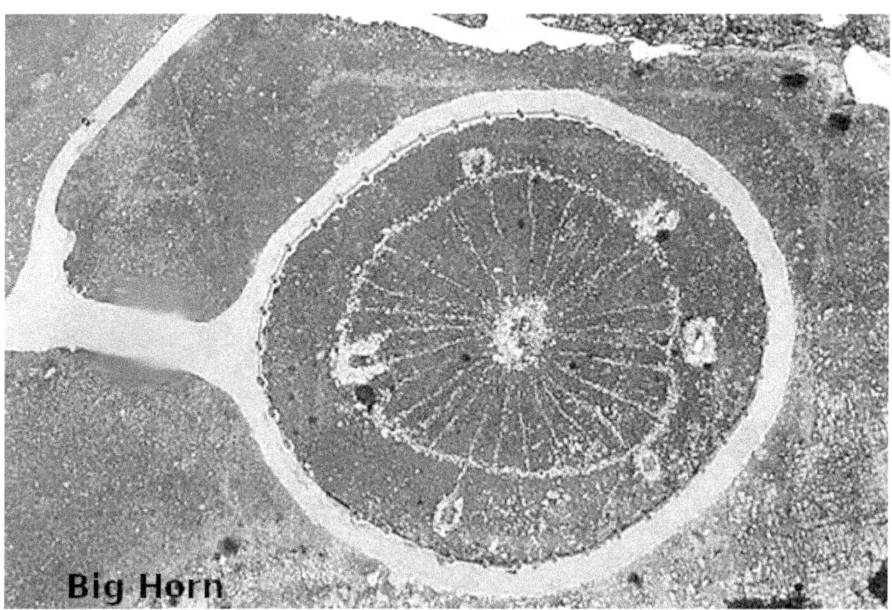

SPIRITUAL LIFE

Animism

Native Americans are animists, which means that they believe that everything that moves (clouds, water, leaves, wind) is alive.

As a result, they live in harmony with nature and have a story for each of its components, such as trees and flowers, birds and animals, the moon and stars. The star looking up is a nenuphar.

The snow that falls from the mantle of Wakinu, the Bear, when it crosses the Bridge of Dead Souls on its way to the Eternal Hunting Lands is known as the Milky Way.

The Pleiades are seven poor children who became stars because of their constant cold and hunger.

Animism in Geography and Climate

In the six worlds of the micmac, located in eastern Canada and northern New England, the same area has life.

Trunks are powers of the natural world, stars are people hunting through the sky, and the Kaqtukwag are people who adopt both human and bird shape. As they fly, their whistle is what causes the noise and the strong winds of the storms beneath them.

Winds are people, just like stations and directions. The mountains, like the lakes and rivers, and the icebergs that float in the sea, have life. The strange aspects of the landscape are people who are thought of with affection or who can be comforted with gifts.

In some stories, cliffs and rocks appear as "transformable beings" who choose these ways to hide or rest. When Ki'kwa'ju discovers that the rock he has bothered begins to roll behind him, ravaging the forest in his way, he discovers these rocks can be powerful and terrible beings.

The grass is the stone of the thunder that falls from the sky in the form of balls or even as arrowheads or spears. A giant that lives in the limits of our world creates cold, windy winds as he takes the snow and ice out of his home with a stick.

Shamans and healers

Only the shaman can talk to the gods or spirits, exchange information with ordinary mortals, and communicate with the souls of the dead on behalf of the living. The shaman is generally an exceptional character, both in appearance and in interpretative skills. He can be a poet, a mystic, a sage, a doctor, a guardian of the tribe, and a storyteller.

The person must "receive the call", live a religious experience and be initiated into the corresponding mysteries in order to become a shaman. His physical and mental pattern completely changes as a result of symbolic death and resurrection. During the period of initiation, the novice perceives the spirits of the universe and leaves his body to travel through the heavens and the underworld as a spirit. In that place, the different spirits will be presented to him and he will find out which of them he should address in subsequent trances.

Individuals who lack all of the shamanic qualities are simply referred to as "doctors or healers". The shaman can take it out and heal the patient because the disease was believed to be caused by a evil spirit that had entered the victim's body. In a special ritual, he does it by playing his drum, balancing and singing, gradually increasing the sound and intercaling it with long sighs, gemstones and hysterical laughter.

The Beyond

In American stories, the existence of a duality in the other world is not common, where one place is placed for punishment and another for rewards.

In the story "Travel to Heaven", narrated by the coushatta tribes of Alabama, the spirit of the deceased must overcome several difficulties.

The most serious problems are a lot of water and a place full of snakes.

They always bury the deceased with a big knife so that he can protect himself from the big eagle that attacks everything that moves along the way.

The crossing under the cloudy sky as it rises and descends to the edge of the earth is the final obstacle.

Death and Life After Death

Indian customs and beliefs about the end of life varied from nation to nation, although many peoples believed that a person had at least two souls. One was material and remained within the body during dreams and illness, while the other was free and left the body in dreams or illness. The first soul was transferred to the future life upon death, while the second soul died with the body or, at least, remained united to it for an indefinite period.

For the Navajo, death occurred when the wind of life entering the body at birth escaped. In general, they feared death because, although the goodness of the deceased helped to balance and harmonize the universe, the negative qualities persisted in the form of a spectrum that could harm the living.

Among the tlingits of the northwest coast, the funeral rites were carried out by another group without any related relations because the most threatened beings by the dead were those to whom they had been closest in life. The Aborigines, as in other transitional rituals, placed the dead in a remote place and cut off their connections with the world of the living. The deceased's house was burned by the Yumas of the southwest, and if the relatives continued to live in the house, they created a door or hole so that the deceived could not enter. The bodies were incinerated, buried in a mound of land or placed on an open-air stand. According to the Lakotas, wanagi spirits, or "shadow things", protect tombs and have the ability to cause harm if the deceased are disturbed.

Almost all nations had faith in future life, although it was not always limited to the stereotyped "happy hunting territory" where the Indians died. One of the souls of the deceased was supposed to meet with the Creator over time. The Delawar believed that the material soul had to go through twelve cosmic layers before reaching it. Many times, the other world was a precursor to the reincarnation of the soul. As the rivers flowed backwards, the seasons mixed, and people danced with their legs crossed, in some villages future life was equivalent to the reversal of the world of the living.

The dead struggled to alleviate their pain because they were often distressed by being separated from the living. Some Indians inflicted tails on themselves or ripped off the jewel from their fingers to demonstrate how much they missed someone. Many people were in a state of mourning for a period of time, while others performed simple and delicate ceremonies, such as the offering of food, in order to facilitate the transition from the deceased to the other world. Some villages, such as the hopis brides, prepared for death from their youth.

The Origin of Death

In some myths about the origin of death, there is a conversation between two beings, as in the following story about the slopes of the Western Plains.

In the past, the two most prominent characters were the Wolf and the Coyote, who always tried to break the plans of the former. One day, the Wolf told him that when a person died, he could be restored to life by firing a arrow on the ground that was underneath him. The Coyote told him it didn't seem like a good idea because if all the people were to get back to life, there would be too many people in the world.

Although the Wolf accepted his reasoning, he decided that the Coyote's son would be the first to die, and his desire was responsible for the young man's death. The Coyote approached him, told him what had happened and reminded him that people could revive by firing a arrow under them. However, the Wolf replied with the Coyote's assertion that the individual should die, and has been so ever since.

The Other World

People describe the beyond as a place full of peace and happiness, in addition to abundant hunting, so they call it "Happy Hunting Places". Because many tribes do not have a lower world or hell, death does not cause much fear. After death, the person can only travel to the land of spirits and live there as he had done on earth.

There are several ways in which living beings can travel to the other world. Some cross a river, a sea or the rainbow. Semi-gods help mortals cross a magic string of arrows or a tree that leads to the upper world. Some people just close their eyes and want to be there.

There are many stories about men from beyond who fall in love with earth women, look for them, have a child and then return home. Almost always, the earthly wife violates a taboo and must return with her child through a leather rope or ribbon. One story of Blackfoot talks about a successful marriage in which the tipis of the different children are seen in the sky as the Milky Way.

The quest for vision

The quest for vision alone is the most common method for many tribes to connect with spirits and gain their power. They can seek it several times throughout life and even at old age, although it is traditionally given among young people. The upper skagit of the western sector of the state of Washington believe that spirits communicate at any age, although by tradition, parents send their children in search of visions from the age of four until puberty. Almost all Indian nations consider it crucial for girls and boys to experience vision and develop spiritual powers.

The individual must purify himself internally and externally through solitary fasting and bathing in the sweat shelter to receive the spirits. The power of the spirit in question is directly related to the duration of fasting.

A culminating stage in the search for visions was the ritual purification that was carried out in the sweat shelter. The individual settled in the shelter and generated heat by sprinkling water on the stones that had been heated; it was impregnated with steam and the sweat was washed by the use of mice. Sweat shelters continue to be used not only for spiritual purposes, but also for the purpose of relaxing and recovering.

Children are instructed about the spirit they must seek. For example, you can tell a child that I have a bow to help him find the vision of a hunter spirit. If the child ends up successful, he should refrain from publicly recognizing it until he reaches a certain age. It is crucial that young people receive only the help of the power they have recently acquired in extreme situations.

The Spiritual Journey

According to many American Aboriginal traditions, some people will never cross the inaccurate boundary that divides the world from the spirits of the human world. However, those who have special abilities or a characteristic that is valued in the spiritual world do not face this difficulty. Some groups fear the spirit world and strive to avoid it; on the other hand, others actively seek the contact and powers it conferred, while a third group believes that the power of spirits arises naturally.

Spiritual power is a mysterious force that comes from everything that exists in nature. According to the few Indian groups describing it, it is intangible and emits an intense white light comparable to the sun. They believe that those who possess spiritual powers are strong and skillful, while those who lack them are ineffective and weak.

It is often said that spirits and spiritual strength appear in visions. Most people seek these alone, especially among the natives of the plains. Participants in rituals such as sun dance can also receive vision through ritual purification, fasting, or physical suffering. As for the millennial movements such as the Dance of Spirits, some people manage to perceive a vision superior to that of today's world by being physically exhausted during dances. The ingestion of peyote along with chants and tambourines can also cause visions.

Sometimes, power arises from having an object in possession. For example, many Indians in the plains and the southwest believed that the shield, made with the help of a sacred being and with a circular structure and coated in leather, represented the world and attracted the protection of spirits. To increase their power, they decorated the shield with feathers or other sacred objects or drew symbols that represented images of dreams or visions. The protective capacity of the shield was also affected by the manufacturing process.

Almost always spirits appeared in dreams that were not sought. Groups such as the southwestern Mohawks and the northeastern Iroquois believe that dreams can direct the power that emanates directly from the spiritual world and reaches the individual. All the dreams were important to the menominis of the Great Lakes region and respected literally the prophecies or warnings they contained. For example, if a person often dreamed that he was drowning, he chose a small canoe as a talisman and always carried it with him. If someone did not understand the meaning of the dream, he resorted to the interpretation of an elderly man because he was closer to the end of his life and was closest to the spirit world. He who did not dream or had a dream impossible to understand was considered isolated from the power of spirits.

The memory of the past

Virtually all the rituals of the North American Indians evoke the past, although they do not always exalt specific events as impressive or exceptional. Western events, such as the celebration of Independence Day, usually commemorate specific events from a recent or distant past that, in any case, are distant from the present.

Native ceremonies and rituals recognize something more than the context in which they are carried out or the representation of the sacred events they include. In line with the traditional idea of "living past," they honor the past as a present, invisible presence that has an impact on people's lives.

Ritual recognitions of the past can be extremely simple, individual and personal. For example, sacred Western shoshon women get up before sunrise and pray looking east every morning. Each prayer ends with the phrase: "Now bless the people." The short "now, then" symbolizes gratitude for sustaining your existence, understanding the natural cycles and remembering your people's past and path to the future.

Some celebrations, such as potlatch, take the form of traditional community festivals. The songs, dances and sacred rites that make up the potlatch of the kwakiutl have barely changed over the centuries. It also represented the shift of power from one generation to another for many centuries. The new leader is given valuable material objects, such as a large copper bar with a representation of a totemic animal, as a sign of his power and what his ancestors and other beings of the past have transmitted to him.

Other memories combine old elements with new forms. The annual Choctaw Fair, which takes place every summer at the Pearl River Reserve in Mississippi, is an example of celebrating the descendants of those who refused to abandon their ancestral lands in the 19th century. Choctaws across the United States gather to remember their history, traditions, and the way they survived as a nation. This fair, which takes place at about the same time that the choctaws celebrated a ceremony in honour of the maize ripening, includes stories, dances and the traditional ball game known as ishtaboli.

Although relatively new, the Indian-Esquimal Olympic Games, held in Fairbanks, Alaska, each year, include ancient elements. The nodule jump, an exercise in which participants jump on the ground, backed on the nodules while imitating the movements of a fox lying on an ice tap, is one of the traditional activities that takes place during the four days of the program. Many spectators and participants are Inuit and urban Indians, for whom games and accompanying activities are a fundamental way to connect with traditional culture.

Transformation into something sacred

Adult foxes actively sought the ability to have visions. They were subjected to physical deprivation and even torture so that they could see. If they succeeded, they hoped to acquire special wealth or powers on the battlefield. Failure was not a social stigma because most of those who tried had never had a vision.

The washos of the Great Basin considered that sacred power came without seeking it or desiring it. The first signs appeared in a series of dreams in which an animal or a spectrum used to appear. This vision gave them powers that would last a lifetime. This power was feared by the washos because it was dangerous and, the more defined it was, the greater risk it entailed. The individual could reject the offering, but in this case, the spiritual being or wegaleyo used to punish the dreamer with difficulties. The wegaleyo gave him instructions through dreams when the individual finally gave in. In particular, he conveyed his unique sacred song or song, the objects he was to use in ceremonies, and the location of the secret pond for ritual ablutions and other sacred practices. The spiritual being required the individual to seek a known sacred person to teach him the arts of hand games, ventriloquia, and other skills necessary for ceremonies.

The upper skagit in the state of Washington believed that shamans were only known when they began to exercise their powers in public. After acquiring the necessary spirits through fasting or visions, each individual decided whether or not to become a shaman. Many sacred beings of this people hoped to mature for spiritual powers, as they could inherit the shamanic spirit of a deceased parent or brother.

The Shaman's Call

A British Columbia kuakiutl shaman tells his personal myth and the visionary encounter that his shamanic powers give him in this short story. We all suffered from virulence, and I thought he was dead. The wolves walked into the tent, grumbling and whistling, and I woke up. Two of them caressed my body as they expelled foam and tried to cover me with it, removing my ribs. The wolves rested when night fell.

I spent the night lying on a pizzeria while dragging me there. It was cold. The two wolves sat next to me, one on each side, and licked me again in the morning. Arponero-Corpo, a figure that had appeared in a previous dream, expelled foam as he pressed his nose against my sternum.

In a dream, he felt a magical power over me and laughed as I said, "Friend, be careful of the shamanic power that has come to you." Now you have the ability to heal the sick and sick those of your tribe that you want to die. Everybody's gonna see you scared.

The relationship between humans and animals

Stories about spirits show people's fear of the unknown, while in stories about animals, people often have a close connection with them, even though they are hunted, they are not enemies of the tribe.

Even the death of a hunted animal is not considered an offence because the animal agreed to be the guest. When a hunter kills an animal, he is praised and told not to be offended, to return the hunter in a different way.

To this, hunters must make sacrifices, such as cutting parts of the animal's butt and throwing them to the ground or the river, while thanking the animal and asking him to come back.

The elderly women tell the children some stories about animals so they can get to know them. The myth answers children's curious questions about their shape, size, or color.

The world is renewing.

For many Native Americans, the rhythms of the universe are similar to those of a continuous drum, as they only repeat and renew as they are played. The rhythms and cycles of nature require human participation through rituals that mark important moments of the cosmic cycle to renew.

Spring and other important dates in the agricultural calendar present a lot of renewal rituals. The southwestern O'odham to-hons (papages) celebrate the saguaro watermelon festival in June or July to prepare for the arrival of rains. To encourage the spirits to fill them with rain water, the pulp of the harvested fruit is collected in baskets and the skins are deposited face up on the ground. The females store the fruit in bottles and store it for storage, while the rest is ingested raw. An elderly man performs secret rituals while fermenting the syrup, believing that they turn it into awardient. After several days, the inhabitants of the village gather and perform rituals to invoke the rain, drinking it to invocate the first rains of the season.

The peoples of the plains perform various ceremonies and practices of renewal, such as the dancing with aros, in which the dancer manages several aros to create forms such as sun, moon, eagle or deer and achieves with great skill the metamorphosis from one figure to another. The aros represent the endless cycles of nature and the universal spirit that unites everything.

The Sun Dance, which takes place every year, is the most important renewal ceremony of the plains. The event takes place from late spring to early summer and its main objective is to foster the renewal of the people's faith in the spirits that rule the world. In the past, it was thought that the dance of the sun secured a large number of bisons for the following year. For most peoples in the plains, the sun dance consists of a four-day cycle in which they perform sacred rituals and dances related to the forces of creation, rather than a single representation. Almost all dances are prolonged tests that usually include autoflagellation.

Every day, the dancers fast and dance around a sacred tree. Dancers who opted for the autoflagellation are attached to the tree during the last day by means of leather strips with pinches that are inserted into the deep open cuts in the chest or back. You have to endure this agony during the twenty-four songs of the dance, which last several hours. The exhausted dancers tend to try to get rid of the bonds and take off the pinches at the culmination of the dance. They consider the dance to be successful if the participant experiences a vision during the prolonged resistance test.

The Preservation of the Sacred

The disturbances caused by the Europeans and their American successors were violent, widespread and often very sudden for the Native Americans. The lifestyle of a community could experience a significant change in less than a generation. Populations were decreasing due to new diseases. Many communities were relocated to unknown lands, which did not exist in their sacred histories, and forced relocations altered family life. The displacement sparked conflicts not only with white indigenous peoples, but also between force-united Indian communities forced to fight for increasingly limited resources. The livelihoods of dozens of villages were destroyed by the annihilation of the bison by the white hunters.

In these difficult circumstances, the Indians tried to maintain their traditional customs for as long as possible. But if Indian communities wanted to adapt to the new situation and survive as differentiated cultural entities, change was inevitable. Pan-Indian religious movements emerged recently, some of which were millennial and predicted the end of white rule and a return to the old way of life. For other spiritual movements,ining the intimate relationship between people, nature and spirit was essential for survival, which constituted the basic essence of many native cultures.

The Spiritual Lifestyle

Everything that the Creator has created, whether animated or not, has spirit, according to the traditions of Native Americans. As a result, all things are connected and are sacred.

The relationships between humanity, Mother Earth, other beings and ancestors are very clear. The earth provides food to humans, including the people, and to all other creatures that the Creator put in it. Therefore, people are expected to have respect for the land.

Many animals, known as "quadrupeds", offer their lives voluntarily to provide food and clothing to the people, which implies that the people must respect them. Those who are now alive must respect their ancestors, as their forefathers lived in the realm of spirits.

In order to survive, people must show respect for their living loved ones and provide mutual care.

This complex system of mutual respect is found in the daily life and ritual and ceremonial practices of the Indian peoples.

Each traditional rite and ceremony celebrates the spirit that unites everything on earth and confirms the sacred relationships.

The Foundations of the Sacred

It is incorrect to mention the "religions" or "belief systems" of the North American Aborigines, as these words often refer to an organized spiritual life that is carried out alongside the daily secular life, from which they are distinguished.

It is important to note that in the indigenous communities of the United States, everyday life and spirituality are so interconnected that it is impossible to distinguish between sacred and worldly. Indian sacred life goes beyond community festivities and ceremonies that mark the annual rhythms and rituals that accompany puberty and other transitional phases. Even the most nimio everyday act has a spiritual meaning for many Indians.

Each Indian nation has its own sacred life and is closely related to its environment. It is based on the sense of community that each village develops in relation to the local landscape and climate, as well as with the beings and spirits that it perceives that live there. However, native traditions share some fundamental ideas and perspectives. It is believed that spiritual power or "medication" is found in things. All plants and animals, even the soil, have a soul that depends on other souls. The seasons and the trajectory of the sun and the moon from one end to the other of the sky are examples of natural cycles that demonstrate the eternal cycle of existence and the timelessness of creation.

Some peoples believe that the powers that sustain the world are manifested in natural phenomena such as winds, rivers, corn and buffaloes. They are regarded as relatives, and the responsibilities associated with these relationships structure community life. Other peoples see the powers of the world as mystical energies and reports, such as the Manitú of the Algonquins, the Wakan of the Lakotas, and the Sila of the Inuit of Baffin Bay.

Each indigenous community carries out its connection with the gods and how it manages and accumulates its "medicine". Some people actively seek the power that allows them to interact directly with spirits, while others acquire it by chance or because of a difficult situation in their lives. On the other hand, it is everyone's responsibility to respect spirits daily as part of their duty as living beings. The definition of good and evil is mainly based on whether or not responsibilities towards spirits are fulfilled. Non-compliance alters the balance and harmony of the world and is a sign of lack of respect. Most of the virtues preached by elders, such as wisdom, courage, generosity, and disengagement, are aimed atining or restoring cosmic balance and ensuring the survival of the community.

Cities dedicated to prayer

Because the Aboriginal lives did not change outside of missions, the task of converting Aborigines was often difficult. For conversion to be effective, the natives had to be isolated from their traditional culture. John Eliot, an English Puritan missionary, brought this idea to an unmistakable point in 1650. In Natick, south of Boston, he established a "red puritan" settlement for the converts, following the principles of his community - a religious colony. The community was built in English style, with a temple and a gateway to cross the river. Locals banned native practices such as polygamy, seasonal migrations, and shamanic cures, and replaced hereditary leadership with representatives elected in the English way.

The idea quickly spread across the coast and another twenty "cities of prayer" were established. They only existed until 1675, when the devastating war between the Puritans and the alliance of wampanoags and narragansets erupted.

The ideas about time

The European imagines the past as a long, straight path that goes back from the present to a distant, invisible place on the horizon. It appears to be a strange place, far from its ancestors, including its own. It is important to note that many indigenous groups believe that time is not linear but circular and is characterized by the birth, development, maturity, death and regeneration of everything that shares the earth: plants, animals and humans. The sunrise and sunset, as well as the solar and lunar cycles, follow this pattern. All things that have completed the cycle live in the past. At present, these situations are present and are not temporary, but persistent.

Whatever their cultural tradition, Native Americans believe that sunrise and sunset are the fundamental rhythm of everyday life, which is what most people believe. Native Americans record the passage of longer periods in a variety of ways and often follow a natural calendar whose markers reflect changes in their environment. For example, while desert inhabitants await the ripening of the fruits of the sage, the salmon's dew is a key seasonal marker for the villages on the northwest coast. In many cultures, the life of communities follows the natural rhythms. It is customary among the Iroquois to celebrate the arrival of spring, summer and autumn with the flowering of the arches (from February to March), the appearance of the first strawberries (in June) and the ripening of the corn harvest (en octubre).

In addition, it is possible that some peoples used the observation of the position of celestial bodies to measure time. It is possible that the mysterious "medical wheels" of the northern plains are used to predict astronomical displacements.

Sacred Societies

Cultures, except for very small ones, are usually organized in groups that are not primarily based on parenting. In the case of North American Aborigines, these groups generally became sacred societies, organizations based on an ideal, ritual, being or sacred object. Although they sometimes had a direct connection with certain clans, there were no structures of kinship between them. Although the individual and his personal ritual life were important, belonging to a sacred society gave the person a more defined social identity. If such societies did not exist or did not function properly, the people felt that their survival was in danger.

Sacred societies received their influence from the spiritual world. For example, some kwakiutl spirits were involved in initiatic rites disguised as dolls or personified. Sometimes, the power of a society was based on a sacred hole of objects entrusted to it by a tribe or clan. Special ceremonies focused on sacred hatches.

Many sacred landmarks for the plain pawnees were closely related to the stars and housed symbols of cosmic forces. In addition, they could symbolize the psychological or fundamental characteristics of the divinity to which the hat was dedicated. The hole could be a piece of leather decorated with stars and wrapped in objects such as scissors, symbolizing the annual renewal of the earth. The skull hole of the Skidi pawnees originally housed the skull of the first man, according to people. Eventually, it broke up and was replaced by a senior official. In the northeast, mainly the societies of curators or healers were highlighted.

Healers' societies were much appreciated by the Hurons because they feared diseases. Each tribe had a leader and the position was passed on from generation to generation; at times, the leader was also an important tribal leader. The Atirenda was a society of healers of eighty people, six of whom were women. The members of the otakrendoiae danced the main dance, in which they simulated killing each other using amulets such as bear sticks, wolf teeth or stones. The main purpose of the atirenda was to cure hernias.

To honor his guardian being, the giant who once challenged the Creator to a test of force consisting of moving a mountain, the members of the Iroquois Society of the False Faces wore the mask of "Torced Face". The mountain struck its opponent in the middle of the face without giving it time to depart, and the giant could barely move it. The giant was excited and decided that from that moment on he would take care of the people's medical care. In any case, his face was completely twisted.

Because they became a convenient way of educating young people and delegating civil and sacred responsibilities, sacred societies were an effective tool of social control. For some tribes, sacred societies were crucial to tribal governance. The Eastern Cherokee of North Carolina, who managed to escape the compulsory relocation of their community to Oklahoma, perfectly combined political activities with the schedule of major religious ceremonies. Tribal officials belonged to one of two societies considered sacred: the White Peace Organization or the Red War Organization. The civil and religious court of the village was composed of the heads of the first, their assistants and seven counselors. Those in charge of carrying out the ritual cycle that included various ceremonies related to corn, as well as those of the "reconciliation", the "new moon" and the "bush jump". In addition, they had civic responsibilities, such as acting as criminal courts, overseeing marriages and divorces, and teaching children how to hunt.

The Red War Organization oversaw all aspects of the war conflict, from the calling of soldiers to the counting of the deceased, and performed purification ceremonies both before and after the battles. The organization was led by a leader who counted on the collaboration of several advisers, healers, messengers and explorers, as well as the involvement of several senior and highly respected matronas, known as the "beautiful women", who played an important role in the development of the war and in the fate of the captives.

There are societies of men and women. The black feet of southern Alberta believed that women were the foundation of humanity and did not perform ceremonies without them. It was their responsibility to keep the sacred hatos, which were necessary to carry out the most relevant ceremonies, such as the dance of the sun. Only women could open the hatches, deliver the sacred objects, and summon the spirits. Before the dance of the sun began, members of the Society of the Old Women built a ceremonial shelter similar to a bison yard. During the fourth day of the ceremony, representations of the entry of the bison into the field were performed, while some of the participants were wearing touches of a bison and imitating it. The celebration of this event was held in honour of the creative spirit, the bison and the history of the people.

Occasionally, sacred organizations were responsible for performing very specific ceremonies.

The Tobacco Society was responsible for the tobacco ceremony, considered essential to the tribe's prosperity in the northwestern plains. The rabbits believed that they could only survive if they continued to plant seeds from the plants they had grown for the first time. The tobacco maker was in charge of the ritual planting that preceded the ceremony. Although it was an inherited position, anyone could acquire the license to become a tobacco maker. The ritual included cutting or burning the arms and chest, as well as refraining from eating and drinking for several days. He would renounce his earthly property in exchange for the honor of planting the seeds.

The Ceremonial Transformations

The Native Americans did not have a clear distinction between the spiritual world and the physical world, as there was an intermediate and transitional third world separating them. To some extent, all creatures lived in the three worlds. A person could become a being from any of the other two worlds if he had the power or performed the appropriate rituals.

Transformations used to mimic the events of the "first time", when the world acquired its identity through cultural heroes and traitors. At ceremonies, someone could take the appearance of one of these figures and think that he was literally transforming into her. A man in sacred black foot really turned into a yellow bear for the gifts.

The supernatural beings that shaped the world in the time of the beginnings used to transform into animals, take human form, or possess people, according to the kwakiutl and haida of the northwest coast. The aforementioned beings were not always just. In some choreographies, two-layer masks, elaborately painted, were used to highlight the alteration. The outer part represented the head of a salmon. During the dance, the dancer pulled out a rope and opened the mask, uncovering the interior that represented sisiutl, a frightening being similar to a dragon. At a certain moment, the mask of an evil being could open and reveal the face of the human being that had been possessed by that being until that moment.

It is very common for men to be transformed into these animals in "animals" ceremonies, such as those of the deer in indigenous peoples. The hunters call the deer in the hills at dawn, and the confused forms of deer men who move as cats astonish at the light of the sun that has just come out whistling cornaments and furrows. The little children, disguised as caterpillars, roam around them while playing and playing in front of the people. The deer dancers are accompanied by a figure known as the mother of hunting.

Food for body and soul: cactus

A physical and spiritual food are the numerous species of cactus that grow in the deserts. In addition, they are a useful source of water in the middle of the desert, and the juice, pulp or fruits are often used during sacred ceremonies.

The pulp is wet under the resistant skin and the dangerous thorns thanks to the water that the plant accumulates as a preparation for the heavy droughts that they usually endure. The juice of the cactus is expressed and drunk fresh. The O'odham spruce boils the sweet juice of the savory until it gets syrup. This syrup is fermented and turned into watermelon, which is used in the annual ceremony to invoke rain.

The peyote is a thornless cactus that grows mainly underground. There is only one round button at the top of it that provides a hallucinogenic drug that is used for ritual and other purposes. The rites of the Native American Church are based on peyote, which is either eaten or drunk.

Shamans

In most Native American traditional cultures, it is crucial to establish a direct link with the world of the gods and spirits. This connection is achieved through the process of "visionary search", which consists of a process of fasting and prayer alone in a remote place, in which a person tries to obtain the vision of a guardian spirit, which usually appears in the form of an animal or natural element.

Those who experience this visionary experience more naturally could ascend to the position of shamans, healing priests and intermediaries between society and the sacred world. Although there are many people who are able to acquire the power of guardian spirits and visionary experiences, only the most powerful shamans can become complete. Those who do not possess all the attributes of the shaman are called "doctors". The path to the state of shaman usually begins when the person (usually a man) falls ill at an early age and experiences a visionary death and resurrection, during which he meets with the spirits and acquires sacred knowledge.

The account of the first encounter with the spirits becomes the personal myth of the shaman because of the relationship that exists between the Shaman and the spirit world. The relevance of this myth lies in the accreditation of the shaman's skills to the tribe, which allow him to locate the hunt, locate lost objects and, above all, heal the sick.

The shaman has the ability to enter a state of trance at his will and to head to the sacred world, where the dead are found. The visible representations of spirits are found in their "medication burden", which includes a number of objects of spiritual significance used in healing rituals. In addition, spirits are also represented in clothes and personal objects and rituals.

The world of the four worlds.

According to the "emergence" myth of the Arizona hopis, at the beginning of the universe there were four worlds, ours and three below, located in caves, and the first beings lived in the lower world.

Two twins came down from the sky with all the plants, hoping that some of them would have enough strength and height for beings to climb through it to the upper world, and when it came to be too crowded and dirty, they discovered that the cane was the best.

After a while, the second cave was overpopulated and the beings climbed up the cave to the third cave. There, the two brother gods discovered fire and, with its light, people built houses and could travel. However, a difficult period came and the population moved to the fourth world, ours, under the leadership of the twins.

The four existing worlds:The Navajo

The knife story of creation refers to an ascending migration across three worlds. The first and darkest place was the home of Begochiddy, the first man, first woman, salt woman, god of fire and coyote. The son of the sun, Begochiddy, created insects, plants and five mountains.

The six beings were tired of this world and ascended to the second by the stem of a junction. There, Begochiddy generated more mountains, clouds, other plants and different forms of life. The sextet was forced to climb the juncture to the third world, where there was light, rivers, springs and abundant life due to conflicts with other beings.

Although Begochiddy created human beings, malicious magic arts caused conflicts between men and women, and Coyote stole the monster's son of water, which, furiously, caused a terrible flood. Although the group tried to climb the juncture again, they failed to reach the next world. With the help of the spider town and Langosta, Begochiddy managed to reach the fourth world, that is, this one, and discovered that it was an island in a great sea. The retreat of the waters was caused by four gods, and the winds dried the ground. At that time, Begochiddy created the world as Navajoes know it.

The gods yei

In Navajo mythology, there is a group of gods called Yei, who play an important role in the creation of the world and are represented in certain healing ceremonies.

The masks used in these ceremonies are created by stifling the deer with corn powder on their cheeks to keep their skin intact. They are made during the ceremony of the Night Song, which is when the young

Navajo learn the secrets of the Yei. The masks are ritually consecrated and brought to life by feeding corn and inhaling smoke.

The Speaking God is the leader of the Yei, who appear individually (in ceremonies) or in groups (en las danzas a las puertas de ta casa de ceremonias u bogan).

Sacred team games

Occasionally, sacred societies specialized in a specific sport. Team games were undoubtedly recreational activities, but they also had a larger social and religious function, like most facets of native life.

The ring and rod game is the most common example. It was a sport practiced mainly by men throughout the American continent that consisted of throwing a spear or arrow at a bow or ring rolling on the ground. The ring was symbolic. In the Zunni version, there was a ring covered by a net that represented the cloth of the ancestral protector known as Woman Spider.

This is a very old game that had a great diversity in the objects used and in the rules. Despite the diversity of players, it seemed that there were always two teams, representing a fundamental duality: "we" (the population) and "they" (las fuerzas ocultas). If you bet, as in the arapaho culture, the winnings were distributed among the members of the team.

Sometimes the time at which the meetings were held was crucial. The Northwest coast wasks, for example, played this game to score the first salmonette of the season.

Humanity's Relatives

Animals play an important role in Native American mythology because they are believed to have a close connection with humans. The myth says that in ancient times, before the change that left them with their present identity occurred, people did not differ from animals and had the ability to transform themselves at their will. Some peoples on the northwest coast claim that their ancestors were animal beings who arrived on the beaches, removed their appearance and became humans, thus establishing the various clans. Many myths about human-animal marriages tell how the two species separated.

The belief is that the bear, which sometimes walks on two legs and has a skeleton similar to that of humans, but larger in size, is the closest animal to man. In several myths, bears are represented as a human-shaped race that publicly exhibits its own skin. According to a northwestern myth, the daughter of a chief named Rhpisunt was collecting berries one day when she encountered two young men who took her to a house where the bear-people lived. Inside was a large-sized man, known as the chief bear, and everywhere were skins of these animals hanging. Rhpisunt married the chief's son and had two sisters.

After a while, Rhpisunt's brothers discovered that the young woman was living in a harbor with her new family. With their children, they returned to their father's village. By removing their skins, the oseznos turned out to be two attractive young people who developed and became great hunters. When Rhpisunt grew old and died, his descendants returned with the bears, and since then, the descendents of Rhpisund have had success in hunting when they remembered the Rhpisun family bears.

According to some rituals and myths, animals are killed and hunted. If the hunters have not complied with the corresponding ritual, there may be a beast master or a shepherd in the tribe who has authority to retain the captured prey. Beasts are considered an important source of spiritual power, and shamans often rely on animal helpers who convey their powers during visionary encounters.

Divine Beings

Almost all American Indians engage in religious practices based on a personal spirit or totem in their daily lives. However, it seems that some communities have a greater connection with the spirit world. The word "shaman" is widely used by anthropologists to refer to these people. A shaman is a specialist in religion who has acquired supernatural powers after being possessed by spirits. It is important to mention that several native inhabitants oppose this expression because they consider it a common expression that comes from a foreign culture, the tunguses, who shepherd reindeer in eastern Siberia, and that does not include the variety of native experts. Per the most appropriate definition is "sacred beings".

Sacred beings range from the person who has a powerful vision to guide him to the future to the skilled practitioner who is in constant communication with spirits and can manipulate the world around him.

Famous warrior leaders such as Sitting Bull and Crazy Horse belong

Crazy Horse Monument

to the first category, and their peoples often regarded them as sacred men. They used their few contacts with the spiritual world for the benefit of the people, especially for war. It is clear that they cannot be called shamans, a more appropriate word to refer to the second category of sacred beings: the person who tries to influence and even impose his will on the supernatural, like the yachi shaman who seeks to transform his body into that of an animal.

Strangers often refer to sacred beings as "magicians," a term that is sometimes used with irony. However, it could be relevant when the visionary capacity of a sacred person relates to the diagnosis and cure of a disease.

Aborigines see sacred beings as a unique point of contact between the natural world and the spiritual world. They generally act for the benefit of the people, but occasionally use their skills to harm people or groups they consider enemies.

Sacred beings have a responsibility to maintain the physical well-being of the population through the prevention, diagnosis and cure of diseases. Diseases have many causes. For example, a disease can be the result of the arts of sorcery or witchcraft. The Western Apaches firmly believed that an incorrect attitude toward the sacred was the cause of some of the most serious diseases. When someone broke the taboos around the things in which they believed the sacred power dwelt, they experienced sickness. For example, eating a deer's tongue, cooking his stomach or separating his tail from his fur were offenses against his power. The rays also caused disease if they walked on a snake's tail or climbed on a tree. The prohibition of urinating in water or defecating in a maize was of obvious practical significance.

When someone in the tribe got sick, they called to the sacred being to find out the reasons and proceed to heal. The Western Apaches performed healing ceremonies. The saint or other elder told stories about the origin of the ritual so that those present could concentrate and reaffirm their faith in the powers in progress. The beginning of the ceremony was impressive, with the lighting of the fireplaces and the sound of the drums. Then the sacred person entered the patient's house, sat by the fireplace and cried for almost two hours while the patient remained immobile. After that, there was a break in which the healer and guests ate and drank tulpai, a fermented corn drink. In the meantime, the sick man worked hard to stay awake. About three o'clock in the morning, the song is repeated to invoke the powers of the black-tailed deer and the beings known as Ga'an. At dawn, the sacred being stopped singing, spraying the pollen of the sword on the patient's head and shoulders, and caressing his forehead with "shining grass." The ceremony came to an end after the sacred person sang two more songs.

In the sub-Arctic, the Tanan atapasks accompanied the sacred being with various spiritual assistants to help heal it. Per he dreamed of natural objects with medicinal properties that he collected and carried in a bag after waking up. The sacred tanana had various ritual "weapons", such as chants, drums, carracas and spiritual masks. Healing consisted of a ritual representation that intimidated the demons that caused the disease. The ability to enter a state of trance and connect with the spirit world was essential to carry out this process. The sacred being, with the help of a specific guardian spirit, determined which spirit had caused the problem and intimidated it by the use of force. Healing often involved removing a solid object from the patient's body, such as a stone, a piece of rope or a projectile. The curator was financed by the patient's family.

Medicinal plants are used by many sacred beings. Although hand games are part of plant healing, it is important to point out that a sacred being is not simply a prestidigitator because it possesses a deep knowledge - acquired through learning - of pharmacologically active herbs and plants with curative effects.

Another type of sacred person is the adivine. Adivining is an esoteric religious practice only performed by some people with special powers. In other words, it is a method to discover things: the guesser discovers the reasons behind witchcraft or sorcery, helps to find something lost or stolen, and predicts the outcome of a hunting game.

Famous warrior leaders such as Sitting Bull and Crazy Horse belong to the first category, and their peoples often regarded them as sacred men. They used their few contacts with the spiritual world for the benefit of the people, especially for war. It is clear that they cannot be called shamans, a more appropriate word to refer to the second category of sacred beings: the person who tries to influence and even impose his will on the supernatural, like the yachi shaman who seeks to transform his body into that of an animal.

Strangers often refer to sacred beings as "magicians," a term that is sometimes used with irony. However, it could be relevant when the visionary capacity of a sacred person relates to the diagnosis and cure of a disease.

Aborigines see sacred beings as a unique point of contact between the natural world and the spiritual world. They generally act for the benefit of the people, but occasionally use their skills to harm people or groups they consider enemies.

Sacred beings have a responsibility to maintain the physical well-being of the population through the prevention, diagnosis and cure of diseases. Diseases have many causes. For example, a disease can be the result of the arts of sorcery or witchcraft. The Western Apaches firmly believed that an incorrect attitude toward the sacred was the cause of some of the most serious diseases. When someone broke the taboos around the things in which they believed the sacred power dwelt, they experienced sickness. For example, eating a deer's tongue, cooking his stomach or separating his tail from his fur were offenses against his power. The rays also caused disease if they walked on a snake's tail or climbed on a tree. The prohibition of urinating in water or defecating in a maize was of obvious practical significance.

When someone in the tribe got sick, they called to the sacred being to find out the reasons and proceed to heal. The Western Apaches performed healing ceremonies. The saint or other elder told stories about the origin of the ritual so that those present could concentrate and reaffirm their faith in the powers in progress. The beginning of the ceremony was impressive, with the lighting of the fireplaces and the sound of the drums. Then the sacred person entered the patient's house, sat by the fireplace and cried for almost two hours while the patient remained immobile. After that, there was a break in which the healer and guests ate and drank tulpai, a fermented corn drink. In the meantime, the sick man worked hard to stay awake. About three o'clock in the morning, the song is repeated to invoke the powers of the black-tailed deer and the beings known as Ga'an. At dawn, the sacred being stopped singing, spraying the pollen of the sword on the patient's head and shoulders, and caressing his forehead with "shining grass." The ceremony came to an end after the sacred person sang two more songs.

In the sub-Arctic, the Tanan atapasks accompanied the sacred being with various spiritual assistants to help heal it. Per he dreamed of natural objects with medicinal properties that he collected and carried in a bag after waking up. The sacred tanana had various ritual "weapons", such as chants, drums, carracas and spiritual masks. Healing consisted of a ritual representation that intimidated the demons that caused the disease. The ability to enter a state of trance and connect with the spirit world was essential to carry out this process. The sacred being, with the help of a specific guardian spirit, determined which spirit had caused the problem and intimidated it by the use of force. Healing often involved removing a solid object from the patient's body, such as a stone, a piece of rope or a projectile. The curator was financed by the patient's family.

Medicinal plants are used by many sacred beings. Although hand games are part of plant healing, it is important to point out that a sacred being is not simply a prestidigitator because it possesses a deep knowledge - acquired through learning - of pharmacologically active herbs and plants with curative effects.

Another type of sacred person is the adivine. Adivining is an esoteric religious practice only performed by some people with special powers. In other words, it is a method to discover things: the guesser discovers the reasons behind witchcraft or sorcery, helps to find something lost or stolen, and predicts the outcome of a hunting game.

The diviner can help the healer find out which taboo the patient has violated and recommend the most appropriate procedure to treat the patient, including the times when the rituals should be performed and the sacred person to be asked for help. The northeastern hurons had three different types of guessers who were highly respected and received a lot of money.

One class found lost objects, others made predictions about future events, and a third group cured diseases. Medical personnel were known as ocata or saokata. Each individual took into account his oki, also known as family spirit, which often informed him about his state of health in dreams. Sometimes, the guesser sought revelation by looking at a glass of water or fire. Some experienced an attack of madness, slept in fasting or took refuge in the sweat shelter in the dark.

The most common technique of guessing among Navajoes is "hand shaking". When someone is sick, an intermediary, usually a relative of the patient, connects with the sacred being known as the "hand shaker", scheduling the time of the visit and offering the cost of the tour. The shaker is placed next to the patient. After cleaning hands and arms, he collects pollen and places it on the feet, knees, palms of hands, chest, between the shoulders, on the coronilla and on the patient's mouth, moving from right to left. The guess is placed a meter to the right of the patient afterwards. More pollen is extracted from the inner vein of your right elbow and extends through the arm to the thumbs of your fingers. While completing this task, he says the following: "Monster of Black Wire, inform me about the state of health of this patient." If you tell me what disease affects him, I'll give you a punishment bill. Repeat the sentence with each finger and assign a different color to the Gila monster (a type of saury) and the number. Then he sings the "song of the monster of Gila", while his arm and hand are shaken, sometimes violently. When this technique is used for purposes other than the diagnosis of diseases, the client is not present; the guesser interprets the trembling to obtain the information sought. A piece of cloth is used when things are lost. In the case of theft, the guesser can be taken to the culprit and grabbed by the shoulder.

Dreams

In almost all Indian traditions, dreams and visions are very important and have helped indigenous peoples a lot when they faced the consequences of the White invasion. Dreams are seen as a source of spiritual power that can be used to obtain information and wisdom or to predict the future.

The Beaver Indians, an Atapasca-speaking village that lived on the Peace River of British Columbia and Alberta, believed that even a young child's dreams were important. However, the most valuable dreams were those a person had when he went out in search of a vision carrying a personal sacred hole. The hole was supposed to hang in the place where its owner slept, and it was believed to have great power over his dreams.

Sometimes, someone dreamed songs that became personal property, or were exposed to personal taboos that prohibited certain foods or activities. Prophets could also dream about things that would happen in the future, and dreams could be used as a defense against witchcraft. Dreams were usually interpreted by an old man or a wizard, who helped the dreamer to understand their meanings.

It is difficult to distinguish dreams from visionary experiences that occur in states of unconsciousness other than sleep. For example, it is difficult to determine whether what Black Alce described was a real dream or a vision occurred during a coma caused by the disease. Sometimes, when looking for a vision, a person may experience a "dream".

Dreams are often related to a person's everyday life, but sometimes they can give access to issues that are important to an entire people. After the whites caused physical and moral harm to the natives, the dreams inspired numerous movements that sought to raise the morals of the Indians and find authentically Indian ways of adapting to a radically changed world. Among other things, this happened with the great dreams and visions of the Seneca prophet Beautiful Lake.

It is said that in these prophetic visions, the dreamer leaves his body to travel to spiritual worlds full of symbolic images that are beyond human society.

Nature and spirit

Many Aboriginal traditions maintain that nature and spirit are inseparable and interconnected, and that spirits reside in everything and that everything is part of nature. This system is centered on the earth. Most indigenous peoples worship it as the source of the endless cycle of generation, destruction and regeneration that they believe controls everything. The concept of Mother Earth, shared by the Indians, reflects the idea of the earth as a powerful nutritious force, although there is intense debate among scholars to determine whether this image is prior to contact with the whites or is simply a European interpretation.

The idea that the earth would receive human beings is present in many native stories. According to many traditions, humanity has a spiritual origin in the earth, which gave it life in the same way that the soil gives rise to plants. However, peoples do not consider themselves superior to other living or inanimate creatures. All living beings must be responsible and share the earth equally.

This attitude goes against the Judeo-Christian tradition introduced by the missionaries, which claims that God granted mankind the dominion of the earth and of all living beings. Animals are highly revered in Aboriginal traditions, and some peoples believe that they are the creators of the world. For many, the Creator was the "dive of the earth," a turtle or other small animal that extracted clay from the early depths and shaped the Earth from this material. According to a duck tale, Old Coyote made the ground by blowing a small piece of clay that the ducks carried from the bottom of the waters. According to ancestral beliefs, animals have spirit, just like humans, and have a complex mutually beneficial relationship with people, plants, and the earth. Animals are often crucial in teaching humans how to behave. Timers, who often present themselves in the form of animals, transmit important moral lessons to their human neighbours.

The deep respect that each people shows for its region is at the heart of every indigenous culture. The landscape is not only a source of strength and identity, it is also sacred. According to Alfonso Ortiz, a tewa anthropologist, his grandmother advised him that when he felt away from his soul, he should return home, as the four sacred mountains that define the borders of the tewa world would renew him spiritually.

Supernatural Beings

The more southern tribes used to have supernatural beliefs in every creature. Because of this, people were constantly surrounded by supernatural creatures that could be perceived in front of those who walked through the extensive jungles or issued strange sounds to indicate their presence.

A common belief was that man was useless to his environment unless he counted on the help of the magical power of some special being.

Spirits have the capacity to dwell in all things that have social or economic value. You can communicate with them through fasting, mental concentration, self-mutilation and even torture, as well as through sacrifices and offerings, prayers and spells, amulets and fetishes.

Heroes, gods and higher beings

Most Native Americans have a supreme God or Spirit. In the indigenous peoples of Arizona and New Mexico, the term Awonawilo-na (El-that-all-contains) is used; for Oldahoma's pawnee, Tirawa (Heaven's Arc), for British Columbia coastal salisch, Sagalie Tyee, for Canada's northeastern algonquins, Gitchi Manitú, and for Utah's pahutes, the twin brothers Tobats and Shinob.

The everyday affairs of the world are usually in the hands of other gods after the death of these supreme gods.

The stars are figures of heroes looking in the sky. For example, thunderstorms, winds and storms can take human form and can also take animal form. The Thunderbird produces the sound of the thunderbirds and storms the storm by winginging its wings as it flies through the sky. The Lightning of the Throne Bird has a spiritual power that must be avoided or revered.

Heroes who overcome seemingly impossible challenges can be half-gods or ordinary mortals who must face certain trials, such as going to the heavenly world or descending to the land of the dead to rescue a dead young woman. In mythical times, the half-gods cleansed the earth from the primitive monsters.

The Sacred Pipe and the Wakan Tanka

The traditional image of the way of life of Native Americans has been transmitted by the peoples of the plains to the world. They lived in typical communities or shops and depended on major hunting, mainly on the huge herds of buffaloes crossing the extensive meadows from Canada to southern Texas. This way of life flourished in the two centuries following the introduction of the horse by the Spaniards, around 1600, but ended in the 19th century with the arrival of European settlers to the west and the intensive hunting of buffaloes.

Because several peoples, such as the Cheyen, migrated from the east under the pressure of the early European settlers, some myths of the plains resemble those of the forested regions. The belief in a Great Spirit, remote and omnipotent, which receives various names, such as Wakan Tanka among the Lakotas and Tirawa among the Pawnees, is widespread, as in the forests. The Sun, the Moon, the Morning Star, the Wind, and the Thunderbird are some of the elemental deities that convey their abilities.

The mythology of the plains reflects the nature of a landscape without irregularities and dominated by the vastness of the sky. Dancing in honor of the sun was a way to recognize the power of this star, and the Morning Star, which is represented by a young man spreading life on earth, is impatient.

Many myths tell of the human ancestors' encounters with the spirits who conveyed them essential information for hunting and survival, and some explain the origin of important ceremonial objects, such as the "medicine bags" and sacred pipes. In addition, there are many stories about evil and deceptive characters, such as the Old Coyote or the Spider (Inktomi) in the Lakota culture.

Yuukipi

The yuwipi, the healing ceremony of the lackeys, is carried out for specific diagnostic purposes and requires full adherence to ritual forms. Participants, for example, avoid all kinds of contamination, especially contact with menstruating women. They must be prepared and prepared, as any mistake can lead to the failure of the ceremony.

First, blankets and blankets are placed on the windows to prevent light from entering. Helpers wrap the sacred object in a canvas or blanket. In the midst of darkness, spirits appear as rays of light, as if eagles were flying through the room, and those who participate can hear the sound of their wings or perceive their cheeks rubbing.

They assign these spirits to make the ceremony a success. If the yuwipi is wellined, the sacred person sees a vision that reveals the cause or origin of a patient's illness and indicates the appropriate treatment. During the yuwipi, sacred beings who have very clear and intense visions are highly respected.

TRADITIONS, MYTHS, STORIES AND LEGENDS

Narrations

Narrators have always been highly respected in Native American society. Many communities follow the practice of the public offering a gift to the narrator in exchange for a story, whether it be tobacco, meat or other food.

Some stories have certain formalities. Maidus, for example, ask listeners to bow up to be more attentive. Cheyenne narrators clean the floor and then rub the body. Sometimes the narrative is preceded by songs or sentences that are pronounced in a language that the audience does not understand.

Stories used to start with a conventional expression, similar to the phrase "Erase once...". The Seneca's tales began with "When the world was new..." while the Zuni started with "Now we dedicate ourselves to..."

The views of the narrators also varied. Some remained seated and relied on the inflexions of their voice to convey emotions, while others assumed the role of characters in the story and used a combination of tone of voice, movements and gestures.

The views of the narrators also varied. Some remained seated and relied on the inflexions of their voice to convey emotions, while others assumed the role of characters in the story and used a combination of tone of voice, movements and ademas.

The legend of the okanagan and shuswap tribes in Canada

A long time ago, when the world was young, animals like the eagle, the bear, the deer, the fox, the coyote and others lived together in peace and harmony. The coyote lived alone in a beautiful place with no friends to share his loneliness with. He found himself so alone that he decided to invite all his friends to a great party that he planned to repeat once a year if everything went well. Then he began to work and quickly built on the river until he reached a waterfall; he hung a boiler on it; he built a trap for fish; and he made a stone seat next to the waterfall to see how the fish fell into its trap and were cooked in the boiler.

The coyote called his friends to go to his party when the time came, and soon everyone confirmed his attendance. They were impressed by the artifact that the coyote had built by the river. They camped next to the waterfall, as everything had gone as planned. The coyote prepared a trap for the salmon, cooked them with rum in his kettle, and they danced and had fun with their games. When the party ended, all the friends said goodbye, expressed their gratitude to the host and promised to come back the following year.

What's the reason behind the porcupine quills ornament?

The messenger of survival: harvest or hunting is the spinning pig.

Pigs-spiders didn't have fists in the beginning of time, when the world was young. In a forest, a bear wanted to eat the dough of the spinach pig, but the pig took refuge in the cup of a tree. The next day, the spinning pig realized how the thorns bothered him, and he had a great idea. He took a few branches of thorns, put them on his shoulder to cover himself and waited. The bear jumped onto him and wrinkled like a ball. Injuring himself with thorns, the bear had to resign.

Nanabozho, who had witnessed what had happened, called the pig spino and questioned him how he had learned that cunning. The spinning pig replied that after having suffered punches on his body, he thought he could use them as a weapon, as he did not want to continue being the victim of the bear.

Nanabozho took some branches of the thorn and mixed it with clay on the spine pig's shoulder, clawing his thorns into the clay and turning it into part of his skin. On returning to the forest, the wolf appeared and, unaware of his fate, attacked the little animal and wounded himself with his thorns. When the bear saw the spinning pig, he didn't come near, because he knew how his weapon worked. As a result, all thorn pigs have lice.

Mocking and mischievous

The most famous character in American mythology is the scoundrel or cunning. Combining human and animal traits, he is a graceful figure, a guasson, an allocated creed and the creator of the universe. The narratives of the Cuervo on the northern Pacific coast and the cycles of the Coyote in the large plains demonstrate this characteristic.

The embalmer can take a variety of shapes: it is the Winnabago's Big Hare of Wisconsin; it is Nanbush or Glooskap (Gluskap) in the north and east of North America (forest zone); it is Rabbit in the southeast; it's Spider in part of the large plains; and it is Vison or Blue Riding on the northeast coast. Whatever form is chosen, the trickster gives the storyteller a lot of action and mimicry, which explains why these stories have been widely disseminated.

This character is a transformator, god and buffalo at the same time in the Cuervo cycle. His insatiable appetite leads him to steal food from animals. Moreover, he is a woman who cannot be cured, although he often feels frustrated in his search.

However, like Coyote, he is often innovative and essential to the tribe. As a result, the name of the haida for the Horn is El-that-should-be-obeyed.

Salmon and coyote

Coyote could change shape whenever I wanted. He fell into the water one day while crossing a river. It became a wooden board to avoid drowning and was dragged down water to reach a dike.

An old woman saw the timber and thought it could serve as a fish dish. She took it home and ate it with salmon. When the salmon disappeared so quickly that it could hardly taste a bite, it is easy to imagine its surprise. He threw the timber into the fire because he was so angry.

Coyote became a baby crying of pain when he found himself in the middle of the fire. The woman quickly pulled him out of the flames and took care of him as if it were her own.

As time passed and the boy grew older, the boy remained as bold and rebellious as he was when he was a child. One day, the woman was forced to leave, but before leaving, she asked the coyote boy not to open any boxes in the warehouse.

Coyote made a promise, but he didn't intend to fulfil it because he was disobedient. I was curious to know what was inside. However, he first tried to break the dike that had hindered his access to the sea. The country of Coyote had no salmon and wanted its inhabitants, who lived in the waters above, to be able to taste it. That's why I had to break the dick so that the salmon could rise.

Coyote broke the barrier with a hammer as soon as the old lady left, leaving the salmon free.

He began to open the four boxes to satisfy his curiosity. Unfortunately, the first formed a group of horrifying vespers; the second, a large number of dark salmon flies; the third, a lot of dark mossardons; and the fourth, a bunch of carnivorous squirrels. From that day on, Coyote could give his people as much salmon as he wanted. However, due to its lack of obedience, its population is now besieged by insects such as whips, flies, mosquitoes and squirrels. Each year they reach their peak during the spring, when the salmon begins to grow in the rivers.

The crown symbolizes light

Whenever they directed their travels toward supernatural beings, the timid heroes were useful to mankind. According to a tsimshian tale, Txamsem (Crown) creates a trap to steal from the heavenly leader his most precious possession, the moon, with the aim that the inhabitants of the world, who until that moment have lived in a kind of eternal darkness, get the light (since the moon is regarded as the source of all light). It is said that the daughter of the heavenly chief drank from the jar where Cuervo became a pine needle.

She consumed her, became a mother and gave birth to a child in the shape of a Crow. Cuervo joined the heavenly chief's family and persuaded the latter to allow him to play with a ball created with a bladder, a container where the moon was stored. One day, the family stopped looking at the boy, and the boy drove the ball back and forth through the door. Dressed in his old crown clothes, he returned flying into the human world with a bladder in his hand. Later, Cuervo asked a group of spectral entities to give him some of the fish he had caught. After they refused, Cuervo became angry and broke his bladder because he was aware of the great opposition of spectral beings to light. The first dawn occurred when the bladder broke, the moon escaped, and light flooded the sky.

The king of the heavens is the thunderbird.

The Throne Ave is the way in which the Throne Spirit appears on earth.

This large animal, which has an eagle-like appearance, emits flames through its tip or eyes, and when it beats its wings, it generates noises. He is attributed to impressive creative and destructive abilities.

Wakinyan, the Lakota Trueno Ave, is a helper god, a manifestation of the supreme being, and there is a cult associated with the personal experience of meeting him. According to the Iroquois, he adopts a human appearance as the Son, the Spirit of the Throne that protects the sky. Among the main gods of the sky on the northwest coast is the Ave Trueno, which is so large that it can catch whales, its favorite prey.

Westerners believe that there are four thunderbirds, each of which lives in a quarter of the world. The Trueno Ave is constantly fighting in this and other areas against the evil beings of the underworld, such as the underwater panther, and its impacts cause the most violent natural phenomena such as earthquakes, floods and storms.

According to local tradition, Native Americans believe that any object touched by the lightning of the Ave Trueno has a spiritual power that should be avoided or venerated.

The Coyote Route

The Coyote is the being in charge of overseeing the "Camino del Coyote", a ceremony to heal the Navajos in which participate disguised representations of the divinities. It is necessary to carry out the ceremony if any member of the tribe suffers from the "coyote disease", which can manifest when one of these animals dies or even when his body is observed.

In the ritual, the patient assumes the role of a hero of a ceremonial myth, sitting on a painting drawn in the sand that represents an episode of the myth and "meeting" the Coyote, who appears as a masked personification. The ceremony guarantees the patient's health and restores his harmonious relationship with the Coyote and the world.

The heart of the brave antelope

Navajo Legend

A long time ago, a man was happy. The newlyweds experienced the happiness of having a child. The Council of Elders named him the leader of the tribe for his reputation, courage and honor. He ruled the tribe fairly. The tribe was filled with happiness, peace and harmony. One morning, however, his wife was not awake, so he went to get the shaman of the tribe. He determined that the woman had consumed an unknown venomous plant, which had led her to a constant sleep. The shaman did not answer Antilope's question about the antidote.

Since he was unwilling to accept the situation, he approached the oldest leader of the community, who informed him of the presence of a magician who lived in a very hidden cave and cultivated a healing plant that was effective against all kinds of poisons. However, they had in mind that he would not give the plant to anyone because he believed that nobody deserved it. Although he warned him of the dangers he would face on the steep road, Antilope only worried about finding the wizard and his beautiful plant.

On an exhausting journey of several days, he lost consciousness. After recovering it, he had to face a big bear, climb to the top of a waterfall while a wolf seized him, and evade an eagle who was attacking him. Finally, he reached a cave, which was reached by crossing the thin layer of water from the waterfall. In that place, he stumbled upon the wizard and requested the plant to wake his wife. The sorcerer replied, "I have no secrets for you, I know all that you have suffered in your way, and I know that the gods stood by you and gave you the speed of the guepard to escape the bear that was chasing you; then, they gave you a coyote's ability to defeat the eagle; and finally, gave you an eagle's sight." "Even though the gods are by your side, don't you think it would be better for them to give you the plant, since you are about to die after your harsh odyssey?" Antilope opposed this. Antilope, so admired by the gods that they helped him get there, offered his heart to the wizard in exchange for the miraculous powers of his cultivation. The sorcerer replied that only he had managed to earn his powers so far because he had a pure and honest heart.

He offered to accompany him to his place of residence to treat his wife. The wizard leads the leader of his tribe through a hidden path that only he knew. By giving the woman of Antilope the aroma of the miracle plant, she awoke from her deep sleep as the magic wizard disappeared on the horizon.

The bear

Because of its apparent resemblance to man, the bear is an important character in North American narratives.

The bear is the animal whose soul is most similar to that of man and can understand both human language and the language of other animals. It is believed that the micmac are descendants of the bear, and the chippewa call it "old man with skin", "woman of the forest" or "wife of the hills".

Canadian ojibwa also see the bear as a woman and associate it with the rule. When the time of the first period arrives, the girls are given the name wemukowe, which literally means "who will become a bear", and during their time in solitude, mukowe means "she is a Bear".

In many myths, the bear is described as a human-shaped breed (often he walks upright and his skeleton resembles that of a man), but always carries his skins out of the house. There are many stories about a girl who travels with an attractive young man, but who realizes that he lives in a village of bears. She marries the young man, gives birth to two twins and returns to her village, where the twins take off their leather coats and turn into two beautiful young men with good luck in hunting.

The thunderbird.

It is understandable that many myths interpret atmospheric weather fantastically in such an element-dependent environment. Many tribes believe that the trumpet is a powerful bird whose eyes and peak emit flashes and whose whistles are as loud as a trumpet.

Wakinyan, the Bird of the Throne, is considered by the Lakots as an auxiliary deity and a representation of the Supreme Being, possessing terrible powers of creation and destruction. For the Iroquois, this eagle-shaped creature adopts a human form as a child, the spirit of the thunder and guardian of the heavens.

Tribes in western North America believe that every end of the world has one of these thunderbirds. The Battle of the Thunderbird is said to cause earthquakes, floods and terrible storms because it constantly fights evil spirits and monsters.

The northwestern Tsim Shians make a wooden bird statue and place it on a large post outside their shops. This image is believed to protect the soul of the shaman, who can encounter many dangers during his flight in heaven. The stone ropes of the Thunderbird stitch the trees damaged by lightning, demonstrating their power.

Windigo

Many indigenous cultures of the United States tell stories about terrifying beings capable of causing harm and death, which are often defeated by cultural heroes. Windigos are giant ice monsters that are mentioned by the ojibwas and northern cris.

Even in the boreal forests rich in hunting animals, a person can become a windigo if he is forced to eat human meat to avoid starving. The death of a windig was seen as a truly heroic act, and often the spirits came to the hero's aid. The monster had long sharp eyes, sharp teeth, and his cry was louder than the tallest trees.

The windigo harassed the hunters while chasing the alps and other lonely animals. The Indians believed that the windig's insatiable greed for human flesh had killed the hunters who did not return to the camp. The evil being could threaten from the forest disguised as indigenous and all strangers arriving in the village were observed with great care and suspicion.

Windigos' stories are very popular and are told as a form of entertainment, similar to ghost stories among non-indigenous peoples. They are sometimes used to re-impose discipline on rebellious children. In the past, Indian children played a hiding game in which a windigo was believed to cover his head with leaves and hide.

Scammers combine entertainment and wickedness.

The supernatural cultural heroes of American mythology can also be liars who use their cunning to steal fire, destroy monsters, and make jokes. In several villages, these tales form a unique mythological unit, and in certain areas, such as the northwest coast, the trickster and the cultural hero are thought of as two distinct people. Tricks myths give the narrator a wide range of possibilities and are undoubtedly the most popular stories among Native Americans. After the slaves of West Africa merged it with a Hare character, one character, the Southeast Rabbit, went into modern American tradition as the Brer Rabbit.

In most cases, the trickster and the cultural hero are named by the same name, such as the Great Hare, Nanabush or Gluskap in the forested area, Rabbit in the southeast, Coyote in the plains and the west, Spider in some areas of the plain and Cuervo, Blue Riding or Vison on the northwest coast. Although it has diverse appearances, it shares common traits throughout the continent and similar stories can be found in distant regions of each other. He can be a skilled joker or hooker and ends up trapped in his own game, wounded or even dead, to reappear with an equally reckless attitude despite the experience. Sometimes, this figure acts irreverently and stupidly, highlighting the importance of moral rules and limits, and many of the myths in which he appears are very common.Sometimes, the character's role as a cultural hero and deceiver is combined into a single myth, as in the myth in which the Cuervo steals celestial bodies. According to an Algonquin myth, Gluskap brought summer to the icy northern regions.

The clever villain travelled to the south of the country of Winter, where he captured Verano, the leader of the "little people" and took her to the tipi of winter, which melted before her presence. Gluskap then allowed Verano to return to his home.

The painful lesson of the great Hare

The following story of the Wisconsin winebagos illustrates the lack of skill of the swindler (in this case, the Great Hare) and the superficiality of many stories about this character. While she was taking a nap, the Great Hare killed several ducks, put them on a fireplace and asked her son-in-law to watch. The foxes stole a person's flesh, and when she woke up and saw what had happened, the Great Liew approached her anus and asked her angrily, "Didn't I tell you to watch the fire?" I'll give you a lesson! He took a tea and burned the entrance of the anus as he screamed.

The Great Hare walked away, shrieking at her naivety. Along the way, he found a piece of fat. He began to eat it, and it seemed to him very tasty, but suddenly he realized that it was his own intestines, which had gone out of his anus. "How right people are when they call me an idiot!" he exclaimed as he was putting his intestines back. In doing so, he pulled hard to draw wrinkles and curves, resulting in the human anus.

The liberation of wild animals

Before humans arrived, the animals had already been released. Before emigrating to the southwest from Canada, the Navajo were hunters.

Before the creation of humans, the Holy People gathered in the sweat pavilion to discuss how to find all the hunting animals that had disappeared. No one had witnessed the arrival of a dark and mysterious figure into the room. They saw her put on the skin of a horn and fly.

A plan was planned to recover the animals: turn one of them into a puppy and allow the black horn to take it away. The Cuervo grabbed the Dog and led him to the Borde Hill, where the Black God resides, to whom all the hunting animals belong, where their dwellings are located.

The pig-spin, who had a turquoise stick to remove the fire and open the door, was the doorkeeper of the house of the Black God. The Dog struck the door with his stick, and there he saw animals scattered all over the place: the Horn, who disguised himself as the Black God, had gathered them. All the animals fled when they saw the door open.

According to legend, when the first four deer crossed the door, the Dog touched their legs to produce a smell and, as the other animals passed, scratched their fist with the wind to warn them of the smells, which gave rise to the beast's ability to detect the presence of someone far away.

The progenitor of the eagle

An Eskimo legend

An esquimal hunter was so hungry that he shot an eagle to feed himself. However, when he returned home, he felt so bad that he had taken the life of the animal that he cut it off and placed it in a place of honor. Every time he brought some food home, he gave the eagle the first bite.

One day, a twenty-one lost the hunter. Two men found him waiting

himself again in the middle of the ventisca. His return to his village allowed him to tell them about his encounter with the eagle family. In addition, he taught them the dance and, every year, they danced it according to the instructions he had given them. Their nets and traps were always full and they never hunted eagles again.

The sun woman, the spider grandmother and the twins

North America: legend kioiva

Spiders are considered messengers and are always a positive signal, except for poisonous spiders (black spiders, tarantulas, etc.), which indicate that someone is telling lies about their person.

While playing, a girl left a basket with her sister inside hung on a branch of a tree. A red bird sang for the baby from the top of the tree. Attracted by the bird, the girl came out of the basket to catch him. The higher the girl was, the more the tree grew, and the farther the red bird was.

When she arrived at the bird, the young woman was already a woman and had come to the house of the Sun. The Sun turned into a bird. He told her that he had fallen in love with her after seeing her from above. She asked her never to take a specific plant out of the garden when they decided to get married.

She had a son. She spent many hours alone at home and felt desolate at the absence of her family. Out of curiosity, he took the plant that had been forbidden to touch the sun and through the hole he could observe his community. Her nostalgia was so great that she grabbed her son and hung him by the hole with a rope. He began to descend, but suddenly the sun appeared and, when he saw her, he became angry and threw him a ring that cut off the rope. The woman, with her child on her back, threw herself into the vacuum.

The child did not die, since it fell on his mother. Grandma Spider found the child and decided to raise him in her store. The boy grew up and one day, his grandmother gave him the ring of the sun to explain to him what had happened. He told him he would never blow it, but one day the boy threw it and the ring returned to him, dividing it into two identical persons. The grandmother welcomed the two children to her home and when she saw them, she understood what had happened.

The two young men always walked together and one day they met a group of criminals, so they sought refuge in a very dark cave. The brothers were stifled by the smoke that the enemies lit at the door, but by pronouncing a conspiracy that their grandmother had taught them, the smoking was diluted and they were able to get out of the cave when the enemy departed, convinced that they had killed them.

After several walks, the twins found their home and said goodbye to Grandma Spider, who wept sadly, and moved to their mother's village. It is said that one of them went to bathe in the river and became an aquatic animal; the other became a well-known and respected leader, who when concerned about some important matter approaches the bank of the rivers and talks with an Aquatic animal that approaches him.

He works as a human messenger or reference. If an Indian was at a crossroads, he only had to look at the antelope footprints to find the right path.

The stone can tell stories.

An orphan was strong and intelligent. One day, his aunt handed him a bow and arrows with the instruction that he should learn to hunt. Go to the woods and bring food. He got up early the next morning and caught three birds. However, around noon, the tendon that held the feathers of his arrow loosened and leaned onto a flat stone to stretch it.

In an instant, he heard a deep voice saying, "Would you like me to tell you a story?"

I was expecting to see someone, but there was nobody. The voice insisted once again, "Do you want me to tell you a story?"

The child began to feel scared. He looked everywhere, but found nothing. He realized that the voice came from the stone on which he was sitting when he ringed again. Would you like me to tell you a story? The young man questioned the stories.- Stories are events of a long time ago. My stories are like stars that never disappear.

After the stone finished one story, it would begin another.

The child remained attentive all the time, keeping his head bent. The stone suddenly cried out, "Now we will rest." Come back tomorrow and bring the inhabitants of your community to hear my stories. Everyone received a gift.

The boy told everyone what had happened that night, and the next morning people accompanied him into the woods. Before sitting, each put meat, bread or tobacco on the stone.

At the end of the silence, the stone began to tell ancient stories. Some of you will be able to remember all the words, others only a part, and others will remember nothing. Listen carefully.

People bowed their heads to pay attention. The sun had almost set when the stone was finished. "I have already told all my stories," said the stone. You must remember them and pass them on to your children and grandchildren, and always do so. And whenever you ask someone for a story, give them a gift.So it happened. All the wisdom we know comes from the stone.

This is explained by the seneca in the area near the present-day Toronto, Canada. The bones of the earth are stones, so they must be treated with respect.

The Sacred Clowns

Many indigenous groups have specialists known as "sacred castles", who in ceremonies are transformed into absurd figures and cause confusion.

During the mandan ceremony, the figure of the Tonto surprised the public by imitating a male bison in full coupling before being expelled from the village without any remark.

Clowns tried to teach with the bad example. The greed was criticized by the Zunji Koyemshi through his grotesque glutony. The Heyoka lakota was even more absurd: he was riding a horse with his eyes turned back or swimming in ice water and complaining about how hot it was.

Animal Myths

For many tribes, animal hunting was their main occupation and their only way of surviving. It was believed that the difference between humans and animals was minimal and could be overcome. Many stories tell how some animals were people in the past and vice versa. The Navajo say of the bear that was once a hunter or a shaman who became a bear and they talk of a land where people were born in the form of large dogs; even fish are humans who have drowned. The hopi believe that when the castor was human, he was extremely upright with the bow.

Animals and humans can marry, and the children of these unions have human intelligence and animal strength. During the hunt, when a storm forced the hunters to seek refuge, the narrator spoke loudly because animals were believed to also be able to hear stories. Hunters were not interested in domestic animals, such as dogs, goats, horses or chickens, so little was told about these animals, as they were not the object of hunting. Some didn't even have names for these unhunted animals.

The bear, the fox, the wolf, the American glutton and, of course, the horn were the most famous characters in the fairy tales.

Nanabozho

You see a low, rocky promontory that looks like a sleeping man with his hands folded on his chest and his face looking towards the sky as he looks at the blue waters of the Upper Lake. In his time, this Sleeping Giant was a famous creator wizard named Nanabozho.

Nanabozho appeared this way. Citche Manitú, the Great Spirit, sent a teacher to the ojibwa. Nokomis, daughter of the moon, was a wise old woman. The West Wind kidnapped his daughter Wenonah.

Two sons were conceived from that union, however, Wenonah and one of the sons soon moved to the Land of Spirits. Nokomis found a small white rabbit. His little rabbit took him and named him Nanabozho.

Nanabozho is a god of Chippewa culture who protects animals.

The rapids, the waterfall, the boiler and the stone chair can still be seen in the river where the coyote built them for its great party, although this episode occurred long ago.

Nanabozho: Chippewa

According to the Chippewa tradition, God is the protector of animals.

The rapids, the waterfall, the boiler and the stone chair can still be seen in the river where the coyote built them for its great party, although this episode occurred long ago.

Decisions taken by nanabozho:

The legends of the ChippewaWhat's the reason behind the buffalo jellyfish?

In ancient times, the buffalo lacked feathers. He ran through the fields, and the foxes, who were his seagulls, accompanied him as they warned the rest of the smaller animals of the arrival of the most powerful. One day, as they went out, he headed to a place where the smallest birds had fallen to the ground. Despite trying to attract attention and be considered, the birds felt threatened and ignored their presence. Instead, the buffalo footed them with his heavy legs, ignoring their screams and weeping.

However, Nanabozho realized what had happened and lamented the events and misfortune of the unfortunate animals. The worthless man decided to take letters on the matter and make justice before the buffalo, whom he struck with a heavy stick in the shoulders. The buffalo, frightened, hid his head between his shoulders. However, Nanabozho simply expressed: "From today on, you will always wear an elegant garment on your shoulders." And you're gonna be shy with your head.

After seeing the event, the foxes were frightened and, to avoid Nanabozho's fury, searched for holes in the floor to hide inside. Nanabozho found them and punished them by saying that they would live in the cold soil forever because they were cruel to birds.

Since then, the buffaloes have a joroba and the foxes have their madrigueras in holes in the ground.

Little Star

When the Sun got out of her bed one early morning, her beautiful son, Morning Star, expressed to her: "I have fallen in love with a girl from the Blackfoot tribe (black feet) and I love her as my wife."Despite her father's warnings, Morning Star painted her body in bronze, put an eagle pen on her hair, put on her scarlet coat and her bright black mocassins, and presented herself in front of her beloved wife.

He instantly fell in love and agreed to be his wife, leaving his home in the plains and flying to heaven. She fulfilled her word when the Sun warned her that she should never look down, toward her home on earth.

After a period of time, his flower appeared, called Little Star. One day, the Moon sat in his mother-in-law's tipi and asked him why the large iron marble in the center always boiled without fire. The moon indicated to him that it had a source of heat. However, be careful: you should never move the pan. If you do, you will suffer great calamities.

The young woman could not satisfy her curiosity at noon, when the moon was asleep. He approached the pot and pulled it away. She could look through the hole under her, surprised. There was his old dwelling, surrounded by green meadows, flowering sauce trees and canine roses. And he experienced feelings of nostalgia and longing to see his people again.

The Sun, the father of Morning Star, realized his disobedience and ordered him to return to earth with his son. He said to her, "You shall not see your husband again." This will be your punishment for not obeying.

The young woman and her son were wrapped in caribou leather and brought down through the hole under the iron marble with a leather strap. However, before reaching the ground, the boy pulled his head out of his skin and the strap crossed one side of his face. Then the tribe would call him Poia, the Disfigured Face.

He became an ugly and bad-tempered child., and one day he made the decision to go back with his father to remove his scar. After many moons, he came to a rocky shore and saw a path of light stretching out in front of him and crossing the water to reach heaven.

On arriving at his father, he removed his scar and returned to his home to marry the leader's daughter, to whom he felt love.

This is the story of the Blackfoot tribe, which is found in the Albert Plains of Canada.

Why is the polar star still?

The living things are in heaven. They're as restless as the Papuots, traveling through the cosmos and leaving footprints all over the sky. Some stars are animals seeking better pastures, while others are birds traveling to warm climates. His favorite hunting place is the sky.

However, there is one person who doesn't move. It's Qui-am-i Wintook, Polar Star.

Nagah, the sheep of the mountains, long ago found a very high mountain with steep sides and a sharp peak that reached to the clouds. Nagah climbed to the peak. The Great Spirit, Shinob, was in heaven when he saw Nagah lost on the top. He decided to turn the sheep into a seed (star), which would shine in the sky so that everyone could see it.

It would be a guide to all living beings both in heaven and on earth. So it happened. Nagah became the only star that stays in the same place every day. She, unlike the others, is always still, allowing travellers to find their way. And because it is in the northern sky, people called it Qui-am-i Wintook Poot-see, also known as the Polar Star or the Northern Star.

It's a story about the paute, an ancient and prosperous people who now live mainly in Utah.

Totemic posts

In carved wood, mythical figures, often animals (such as the Eagle ancestors) are depicted, who have supported the group and given it authority. These totems were also used as funeral monuments for the deceased, located near the tomb of the leader of the late clan.

Some are located next to a river or lake, allowing visitors to easily see them while sailing on the water. These reminders are usually written by the son and heir of the boss to express his desire to be the boss.

The Haida of the Queen Charlotte and Prince of Wales islands were known for performing these totems.

The almizclerous mouse, diving in the ground

Several peoples believe that the almizclerous mouse is the best divers on earth. The narrative of the later Indian castors demonstrates the diversity of the oral tradition, which contrasts with the "pure" versions for non-Indian readers, as evidenced by the Iroquois narrative mentioned below. In 1968, Peter Cliepesia, from the Prophet River Reserve in British Columbia, told the story of the castors. Castor was ordered by God to swim in search of sand and, failing to do so, resorted to Rat Almizclero. It is known that Almizclero Mouse swings and stays down for a long period of time, reaching a significant depth. I don't think I got to the bottom right away, as it took a long time. They were waiting for him at the top.

In the end, Rat Almizclero returned with a small amount of sand on his leg. He returned and gave the world to God, which has led some to believe that Almizcler Mouse created it. It was created that way.

Before there was no land, but an infinite sea, according to the Iroquois account of the dive of the earth. Above it was a great sacred tree, where humans lived in the heavenly world. The wife of the heavenly leader dreamed that the tree was unrooted; therefore, the leader ripped it out and opened a hole in which the roots were located.

The woman fell through the hole and descended into the world. Two swans caught her, but they couldn't decide where to leave her. Several animals and birds stumbled to collect sediments from the seabed, but failed to do so. The almizclerous mouse tried, and when she returned to the surface, half-dead, she had a little mud in her leg. The turtle loaded the clay into its shell and the soil grew to form a new world, in which the swans gently placed the heavenly woman.

Spider rock, house of the spider woman

The Spider Woman, the goddess of the earth, had her home at the top of the imposing Spider Rock needle, according to the Southwestern Navajoes of the United States.

The column rises 244 meters above the ground of the Chelly Canyon in northeastern Arizona. At different times, the canyon has been inhabited by the ancient settlers of baskets, the ancestors of the Indian villages, the Navajo, the Hopis and some small communities of indigenous villages.

The mythology of the hopi Indians says that the house of the Spider Woman is the portal through which humans emerged from the womb of Mother Earth at the beginning of time. The god of the universe, Sotuknang, created the Spider Woman to help him on earth, according to a hopi tale.

The Indians saw her as an elderly and wise figure to replace Sotuknang. Sometimes he carried people between the two spheres, carrying their souls in a basket that came out of their womb, establishing a bond between the human and divine worlds.

HEROES, RELEVANT PEOPLE

Divinities and Heroes

Native Americans believe that the Great Spirit directs all creation and that the powerful deities and cultural heroes, who liberated the world from chaos and gave human beings the objects and knowledge necessary for survival, are in the hands of the world's day-to-day functioning. They attribute supernatural beings or personifications of the divine, such as the Coyote in the southeast, Nanabush, Gluskap, the Great Liebre, Wisakedyak, in the forested areas, and the horn in the northwest. These cultural heroes can also be evil and deceptive.

Myths about the origin and organization of the heavens are found throughout the United States, often mixed with other myths. The Tsimshian of the northwest coast, for example, say that a greedy chief guarded the celestial bodies until Cuervo stole them, who threw them into the sky, while other peoples tell that the heavens were arranged in a more careful and systematic way.

The supreme spirit Tirawa assigned a position and a portion of his power to each celestial body, according to the pawnee. Shakuru (the Sun) moved east to live there every morning to provide light and heat, while Pah (the Moon) moved west to provide nightlight. The Morning Star, the Evening Star, Death Star and the four that hold the sky were also given positions.

A spider can be a cultural hero, as in the Cherokee myth about fire theft, and often plays an important role in the creation of the world. Fire did not exist at the beginning of time, but one day the god of the thunder sent a lightning to seize the trunk of a hollow sicomoro on an island. The Water Spider woven a small can of cloth and put it behind. He went to the tree, put a scroll in the vessel and gave it to each being.

The logic that death creates space for life and that space on earth is limited is accepted in most accounts of the origins of death.

Native Americans are more concerned about this world than the other, which is often imagined as a place very similar to what we see, but with more hunting, so there are few myths that describe the life of ultratumba. The villages of the plains are known for their "Happy Hunting Land".

Native Americans maintain that the elemental gods and spirits are in charge of the forces of nature, to whom the Great Spirit delegates its various powers, such as the Sun, the Earth, summer, winter, rain, lightning, and the four winds. Thunderstorm is one of the most powerful forces. Many peoples in the plains believe in gods and spirits of the Earth, the Fire, the Water or the Air (the Thunder is a god of the Air), while the foresters divide the Gods and Spirits between those who dwell on the earth and the waters (such as the Thunderbird) and those who live below, usually evil and headed by deities such as panteras or horned snakes. Indigenous deities are divided into two groups: elemental gods and ancestral spirits, known as kachinas. The kachinas serve as intermediaries between humans and the gods and present themselves as masquerading personifications in rituals.

Heroes

The theme of the hero overcoming seemingly unsolvable tasks is a universal theme in mythology all over the world, and this theme is well developed in North America. Heroes tend to be half-gods in some areas, such as the Southwest and California, and their adventures consist of cleaning the land of primitive monsters from mythical times.

However, in most of the continent, stories tell the adventures of extraordinary people in a world similar to the present.

The work of a hero usually takes him to travel to other planets. In the stories in which the purpose of the test is mentioned, the celestial world, the residence of the Sun, or the heavenly leader is generally mentioned. The hero's journey to the land of the dead to bring back the beloved is the subject of another group of stories.

In some stories, the dead wife does not return because a taboo was broken; in others, the deceased woman comes back to life, as in a winnebago tale that, unlike the cheroki story, has a happy ending.

Cultural Heroes

Most of the oral traditions of the North American Indians describe the mysterious beings who created the cosmos from nothing in very imprecise terms. They modeled an empty and informal world in which then the drama of life arose. When the universe began to exist, the most well-known and easy-to-reach beings transformed the yerma earth into a habitable place. Western anthropologists call these individuals "cultural heroes" or "transformers", and often have human or animal personalities and characteristics. They endowed the landscape with its physical form, flora and fauna, and protected the first humans from monsters. They actively participated in human affairs and transmitted the light, fire and tools and techniques of their traditional cultures to the peoples.

Some transformers were generous and heroic beings who protected the first people and their descendants. For example, the penobscot of the northeast tell that the hero Glúskap killed a monstrous frog that caused the drought because he drank all the water in the world. The Northern Attapasks refer to a hero commonly called Castor Man (who some groups call Old, Wise, or Navigator), who fought several cruel giants -- Bear, Gluton, and others -- who intended to devour the early humans. Man Castor always made up his minds to escape the monsters trying to catch him.

Other transformers were the "timers", who were unpredictable, selfish, and perverse people who often caused change in the world due to their risky actions. In the stories of the northwest coast, it is mentioned that the timer Vison faced constant difficulties due to his insatiable sexual desire. It is important to note that most of the transformers of Indian traditions, such as the horn, coyote, white-tailed rabbit and many others, had characteristics of heroes and timers.

According to Native American beliefs, these individuals lived in a sacred past that was not a distant and primordial time, but a living and invisible environment. Westerners find it difficult for us to understand this concept, as it implies that, although they occurred in a linear sequence, the events described in the myths, such as the tsimshian account of the theft of the moon by Cuervo, have not disappeared from the past, but continue to exist, like Cervvo, "out there".

This world of the "present past" houses societies similar to those of animals and humans. They can talk to each other and change shapes according to their preferences. For example, in some tsimshian stories, the Cuervo is a man (or humanoid) who wears the garment of a horn and can remove it to show his human form. In some Apache versions, Coyote, the famous timador hero, appears dressed as an apache, speaking and acting like human beings, although sometimes running cats. Only humans and animals have clearly defined fixed forms in the visible world.

Indians perceive the evidence of this "present past" through visions, dreams and memories perpetuated by oral tradition. Often, the individuals of that age make their presence felt in the material world. For example, a traditional Native American can see lightning as the blinking of a being they call the Thunderbird, and the wind as the roaring whirlwind of their wings every time a storm occurs.

In many native traditions, the Thunderbird is considered a cultural hero, for example, for killing dragon-like aquatic animals or for catching whales to feed needy populations.

The word keeps the stories of heroes and timers alive. The stories are presented in religious and secular contexts, and although they refer to a sacred time, they are not a rigid liturgy in form and content. Different versions may vary significantly. Sometimes, two completely different myths describe the same phenomenon. According to a story by the Californian Washos, a figure known as the Woman of Creation created the tribes of California from sword seeds. According to another story of these Indians, the three sons of the Creation Man argued and fought like the ancestors of the Californian peoples.

Native mythology has been very flexible and open, allowing strong external influences, such as Christianity, to introduce new characters into ancient stories. For example, some stories of timers and transformers of the Northwest Coast salish included Jesus the Traveler in the early twentieth century. This character cultivated the thorns of the fish and taught the village how to make haches, hammer and traps to fish salmon.

Ancient traditions may have been weakened by external factors, but this has not prevented the emergence of new native cultural heroes. The Indians do not distinguish between what Europeans call "mythological" and "historical", so they could be human beings. Dull Knife (Roman Knife), leader of the Northern Cheyenne, is one of the most recent cultural heroes. Dul Knife opposed the relocation of his village to Oklahoma in 1877 and returned to his homeland with 383 sick and almost unarmed Cheyenes. Until he surrendered with his followers in late October 1878, he abandoned the United States army. They were confined to a former Fort Robinson headquarters in Nebraska, and there, on January 9, 1879, Dull Knife began an astonishing escape. Later, many Cheyen were killed, but Dull Knife and his family survived. They were subsequently granted a reserve on the banks of the Tongue River in Montana. Today's northern Cheyenne enthusiastically remember Dull Knife as the savior of the country. They consider their victories as significant and magical as those of Coyote, Cuervo and other heroes who fought against the enemies of the people.

Louise Erdrich

One of the most famous native authors of the present era is the novelist Louise Erdrich, who is the daughter of an ojibwa mother and a German father. His works, which are based on the North Dakota community where he grew up, have been well received in the United States and other countries. Erdrich analyzes a number of current issues facing Native Americans, highlighting the struggle to preserve their Indian identity without being hindered by overwhelming pressure imposed by the predominant white culture.

Love Medicine (1984, awarded the National Prize of the Circle of Literary Critics and the award for best book by the Los Angeles Times), The Beet Queen (1986), Tracks (1988) and The Bingo Palace (1993) are the four volumes of the acclaimed family series that addresses the problem that complicates relationships between generations.

Black Alce

The Holy Man Black Alce (1864-1950) is undoubtedly the most well-known native visionary of North America, thanks to the success of John Neihardt's book Black alce speaks, published in 1923.

He lived at an important time for the Oglalas Sioux, when the confrontation with the White began which resulted in defeat in the Indian wars and began life in the reserve. Alcé Negro was an active member of the Danza de los Espíritus institution and fought to the end for the survival and well-being of his people.

According to Neihardt's book, Black Alce was unconscious for twelve days when he was nine years old in 1873. During this time, he experienced a dream or visions in which two individuals guided him towards the clouds and showed him a black horse called "The Horse of the Four Directions" (north, south, east, and west orientation).

The "six grandparents" were seen by this animal in a cloud in which they represented the six directions (norte, sur, este, oeste, arriba y abajo). Each of the six explained to him some of the important powers that would make him a sacred man, capable of healing diseases and sorrows, and assigned him the task of guiding his community along the sacred Red Way, which was the only way to ensure his survival.

Black Alce is said to have seen great wonders that allowed his people to resist the massacre carried out by the whites.

Big Thunder talks about the earth

Bedagi, a well-known speaker of the wabanakis (the micmac, passamaquoddy, penobscot and maliseet) in the early twentieth century, spoke about nature, birth and death. Although there are variations, the main theme of the speech is obvious: humans, animals and plants are born from the earth, are part of it, and eventually return to their origin. Our Father is the Great Spirit, while our Mother is the Earth, who supplies us with food. It gives us the plants that heal and it returns us what we put into the soil. Yeah, we're hurt. We went to see our mother and we tried to get her to cure us. When we go hunting, it is not our arrow that kills the arrow, but nature, regardless of the power of the bow. The alce turns to our Mother to heal him and support the wound on the ground, but only gets the arrow a little more as it clings to the flank. Meanwhile, I'm following him. The alce disappears from my sight and, as I hold my ear on a tree, I perceive its next leap and I chase it. Every time it stops to rub, your arrow clings a little bit further into the flank. At last I find him, he's exhausted and his body is pierced by a arrow.

The Chief Joseph

Joseph, the chief, was t the early days had a good relationship with the whites. Joseph, whose father initially converted to Syrian Christianity, passively accepted the efforts of the U.S. government to obtain the land they had granted as a reserve in 1855. The village had only a month to return to Idaho and no longer had patience. On 12 June 1877, clashes began.

Although the government forces were superior, Joseph succeeded for three months and demonstrated great military skill and courage by circumventing soldiers and groups of Indian enemies.

Eventually, luck turned him around and, despite being a man of peace, he surrendered on 5 October. It is said that he delivered an emotional and moving speech in which, among other things, he stated: "I will never fight again." However, we are not aware of his precise words, which were embellished by journalists.

Many of his supporters went to Canada. Joseph was transferred to Kansas and then to Oklahoma, Indian territory.

He spent the last days of his life in the state of Washington, where he died.

The Prophet Shawnee

Shawni culture was in danger in the early 19th century. Clashes with the whites were constant, the hunt had been exhausted, and alcohol consumption made things worse.

Lalawethika, the younger brother of Shawni Chief Tecumseh, had a series of visions during an epidemic in 1805. He was once a vague man, drunk and fanfarron, but visions turned him into a different man. It was said that the "Lord of Life" had shown him a paradise full of hunting and cornfields, and that this was the world of the shawnis before the white arrived. This paradise would re-exist if the Shawnis returned to the path of virtue.

Lalawethika taught many traditional shawnis values, but also some that were inspired by Christian doctrine. Some of the virtues he preached were called Tenskwatawa, which is now called Teskwatawa. Tenskwatawa attracted many followers, mostly non-Shawnis, including Tecumseh himself.

In 1807, the followers established a community called the City of the Prophet, which led the United States government to consider the movement dangerous. The prophet confronted the federal troops at Tippicanoe in 1811, against any council. The Shawnis were defeated and Tenskwatawa lost all influence in the coup. Two years later, Tecumseh died in battle, but continued to take care of his brother until the end of his days.

Glooskap and Malsum.

Legend of the Algonquin Indians

Glooskap, the Liar, was praised for his cunning, a virtue that the tribes greatly valued. He had a twin brother named Malsum, the Wolf, who was his opposite and symbolized all evil.

Malsum asked Glooskap how he could die, and the elder brother told him that the only way to kill him was with the touch of a fox's pen. Malsum told Glooskap that he could only die with the root of a frog.

The wicked wolf grabbed a goose with his bow, and while his brother was asleep, he scratched it with a feather he had drawn out of the wing. Glooskap died immediately, but soon resurrected. However, Malsum was determined to kill his brother and destroy him at the first opportunity.

Glooskap headed to the forest and sat near a stream, saying that only a green juncture could kill him. He said it because he knew that the castor was hidden among the junkies, and he would hear everything and then report it to Malsum. The castor revealed to him the secret he thought was his brother's. The wicked Malsum rejoiced so much that he promised the castor to give him whatever he wanted, but he laughed at him when he asked him to have a pigeon's wings. The castor was angry and turned to Glooskap to tell him everything that had happened.

Glooskap took the root of a frog and hurried to find his brother in the depths of the forest, hitting him with the deadly plant.

Iroquois

The society of the Iroquois Indians was a democracy, probably the first in human history, and women were actively involved in domestic and political decisions. The Constitution of the United States of America was written by Benjamin Franklin on the basis of the democratic principles of the Iroquois people.

These refined traditions wereined in the Mississippi culture, which emerged after that of Hopewell in the year 700. The northeastern agricultural societies outside the Mississippi Valley did not practice ritual life on such a large scale. In the inner forests stretching east and south, from Lake Huron to the Apalachian Mountains, a group of peoples with a distinctive language, the Iroquois, formed in the midst of the Algonquin culture that surrounded them. The Iroquois were farmers who used very advanced grinding techniques. Despite their number disadvantage, by the end of the 17th century they had control of the northeast. Most Iroquois-speaking people lived south of the San Lorenzo River, in the present-day north of the state of New York. Another group lived in the lowlands separating the Lakes Huron, Erie and Ontario. The life of the Iroquois was based on villages with long, rectangular houses with cobbled roofs, and in the nearby clear areas they planted mainly corn. Several related families lived in each long house.

Prior to the 15th century, the League or confederation of the five nations of the haudenosaunee was established by five Iroquois tribes: the cayugas, the mohawks, the oneidas, the onondagas and the senecas. The Tuscany nation joined the league in 1714, which extended from the Hudson River to Lake Erie. All six nations dominated the leather trade throughout the 18th century. They conquered the heart of the northeast, sent the Hurons to the north, and forced the Algonquins to relocate to the east and west. The League, as the main Indian power, participated in the colonial conflicts between France and England. Since 1783, he has served as an example to the leaders of the newly established United States thanks to their political cunning, diplomatic skill and domination of a vast and complex territory.

The Seven Dancers of the Iroquois.

A long time ago, a group of seven children established a secret organization: they gathered around the fire at night and danced to the sound of the drums. One day, the little boss proposed to eat at the next meeting in front of the fire. Each one had to ask his mother for some food to bring to the banquet (maize, veal meat, sausages...), but the mothers did not accept it.

The children felt very unhappy because they could not get the food for the night banquet. The little chief told his warriors to dance as loudly as they could and to look into the sky as they did as they gathered by the lake, in their secret place. Furthermore, he ordered them never to look back, even if their parents were shouting to them to go home. He took his drum and played a magical melody. So the youths continued dancing until they felt their bodies ascending to heaven.

Their parents saw them dancing on the trees and told them to come back. One of the young men looked back and became a small, flashing star in the sky, just like the others who were transformed too. Therefore, it is said that small warriors are the stars that creep at night during the cold winter.

Hiawatha, the snake depilator

Conscious of the wars which were slowly destroying his earthly children, the great spirit convened a council to which he convened the bravest of all the tribes. He insulted them for their conflicts and promised that he would send a healer to teach them peace.

Over the years, a boy from the Mohawk tribe had a dream of the Great Spirit one night. The young man had the expectation of a world without war conflicts.

The Iroquois were convinced and formed a tribal league (Ho-de-no-sau-nee) when the boy grew older and tried to share his vision with others. Only the Onondaga, guided by the evil Atotarho, their healer, remained outside the league.

The young man travelled to the territory of the onondaga and sat in front of the camp fire to celebrate the meeting. Despite the agitated snakes covering Atotarho's head, the tribe agreed that the young man would be the leader and the onondaga would be in charge of protecting the sacred fire.

He lifted up the cornamenta of the sacred deer and placed it on Atotarho's head. The snakes fell to the ground, dead, at the astonishment of all. The young man became known as Hy-ent-wat-ha, the Snake Painter, ever since.

The main figures

Aboriginal traditions do not clearly distinguish between what Western anthropology calls mythology, legend, and history. From the Indian point of view, the assessment of the emblematic figures of North America includes mythological figures such as Cuervo, Glúskap, Kokopelli and others, who are recognized as real people who provided important benefits to the people.

It is very difficult to limit the evaluation of leaders to those who have protected the integrity of natives from white attacks. All Aboriginal cultures have praised the wisdom, power, and courage of recent generations of elders, leaders, and sacred beings. The contribution of Aboriginal history to the existence of the natives has been virtually overcome because families and communities were exterminated during the European invasion. There are notable exceptions, such as that of Black Alce, a sacred oglala man who experienced both happiness and pain during the last years of freedom of the Plains Indians.

The most well-known indigenous figures are related to resistance leaders, who opposed European soldiers, settlers, and politicians and their successors in the United States. The descendants of warrior leaders such as Goyathlay (played by Jerome), Sitting Bull, and Chief Joseph and others their accomplishments, which were recorded in official documents and addressed by white journalists, writers and photographers. Most of this phenomenon occurred in the late 19th century, during the Indian Wars of the Plains. However, the first widely known native leader was Wahunsunacock or Powhatan, leader of the tribe of the same name in the early 17th century. After the English established a colony in Virginia in 1607, he established an alliance with the tribes on the southeastern coast and tried to maintain the integrity of his nation. The clever diplomat Powhatan allowed his daughter Pocahontas to marry John Rolfe, an Englishman. He took her to England, where the young woman, aged 21, died of virulence in 1617. Native leaders often realized that, despite following Western patterns, diplomacy was not effective in curbing European usurpation. John Ross, the leader of the Cherokee nation in the 1930s, tried to "civilize" his people in the eyes of white Americans, but was eventually forced to abandon their traditional territories due to the well-known Indian Removal Act of 1830. Ross successfully overturned the order before the Supreme Court, but the decision was ignored and he was part of the last group forced to move west in 1838. He worked hard during the following years to improve the situation of the Cherokee in his new home.

Many leaders, desperate for the loss of their homes and lands, resorted to armed resistance. In 1763, Ottawa leader Pontiac, who was also a great speaker, joined a powerful visionary known as the Delaware prophet and led the northeastern tribes, which included the Delawar, the Huron, the Seneca, and the Ojibwa, to fight against the British. Nearly 2,000 settlers lost their lives when strongholds and factories fell, and Pontiac and his troops besieged Fort Detroit for several months.

Jerome

Jerome (1829-1909), leader of the chiricahuas apaches, is known for his innovative military strategy: his resistance to the whites and his extraordinary guerrilla tactics only came to the minds of the Indians, not those who were not. Born in the south of Atizona, his apache name was Goyathlay, which means "the one who steals", and after several risky incursions, the Mexicans gave him the Spanish name.

In 1859, the Sonora military governor's wife, three children and mother were murdered by his soldiers. Geronimo committed to retaliation and joined Cochise, the leader of the chiricahua apaches. Together, they attacked Sonora and caused the death of many enemy soldiers. In subsequent years, several cities in Mexico were the target of attacks.

Despite his lack of ancestry, he often played the role of spokesman for his community. Jerónimo and other chiricahuas escaped to Mexico after being forcibly transferred to the arid lands of San Carlos in 1876. However, they were arrested and returned to the new reserve. In 1881, he re-attacked and finally surrendered in late 1886. The army moved him to Florida with his supporters and then to Fort Sill, Oklahoma, in 1894. Jerome adopted the profession of rancher. After his death, he attended the Louisiana Acquisition Exhibition in San Luis in 1904, sold souvenirs under his name and a year later participated in the inauguration parade of President Theodore Roosevelt's term in Washington.

Red Cloud

Red Cloud, also known as Makhpyia-luta in sioux, lived between 1822 and 10 December 1909 and was a leader of the Oglala Sioux. He led the war against the United States from 1866 to 1868, also known as the Red Cloud War, to gain Powder River territory in northwest Wyoming and southern Montana.

He was born near the Platte River, near the present-day city of North Platte, Nebraska. His mother was a Sioux Oglala and his father was a brulé. He died very young. Red Cloud's mother-in-law, Chief Smoke, raised him in part. He fought against the nearby pawnee and sioux when he was young, which gave him an exceptional military experience.

The Red Cloud War, the most successful Native American war against the United States, began in 1866. The Bozeman route, which crossed the Lakota territory of Wyoming and Montana, was being built by the U.S. Army. Red Cloud had visions that the Lakots of Minnesota would be expelled in 1862 when settlers and miners began crossing Lakots' territory. Red Cloud attacked in 1863.

Red Blue achieved impressive victories. The Treaty of Fort Laramie of 1868 forced the U.S. government to do so. The United States pledged to abandon the fortresses of the Bozeman route and to acquire the lands of what is now the western half of South Dakota, as well as much of Montana and Wyoming.

White Buffalo and Eagle Eye

Arizona, hopi tradition.

It is one of the most important things in Indian culture and in its spirituality. There is a legend among the Sioux tribes about the "White Buffalo", who gave the Indians the sacred pipe. He considered himself a god and had powers such as strength and the spirit of survival, especially appreciated by the plain tribes.

Eagle Eye was a brave red-skinned boy who wanted to grow up to be able to hunt, but this activity was reserved for older people, who had been trained by an experienced hunter for more than six months. He helped his mother and his brothers by curing the skins or salting them to keep them fresh. But he had also learned how to use the bow and knew how to distinguish the different animal prints.

As a result, Eagle Eye chose to join the group of unknown hunters after the hunters refused to take the young man.

In the morning, he walked behind the hunters in secret, carrying food, water, coat and a sharp oak rod as a weapon. The group of hunters arrived at the hills in the fall of the afternoon to hunt deer and prepared a large fireplace to withstand the cold and cook their food.

Eagle's Eye was dead of cold and hunger because he had forgotten to bring the straw and the stone to be able to put on the fire. I would like to go to the camp, but I was afraid of being punished for not obeying. Suddenly, he heard the roaring of a puma and ran toward the hunting camp. They were angry at the lack of compliance and gave him a loud blast as they laughed at the frightened child.

The chief of the group asked him to stay and take care of the camp while they were hunting the next day. The young man remained in the camp unwillingly and then left a few minutes later. He began to walk when a snowstorm broke out that brought a dense fog. He lost his orientation. Without knowing where he was, he saw the figure of a great white buffalo, a magical and sacred animal for all the tribes of red skin. Although he was afraid, he approached cautiously and the beast led him to his home. The buffalo disappeared into the fog after being protected.

Eagle's Eye came and told them her story, but they didn't take it seriously. However, the chief, who had travelled south, explained that there was an enemy group that killed and destroyed everything he found. They were white-skinned, wore armor, used sabers and rode horses. Eagle Eye's grandfather and his family escaped from this enemy during a cold winter, but were lost without the food necessary to survive, so the grandfather decided to hunt an animal to relieve his hunger.

They were white-skinned, wore armor, used sabers and rode horses. Eagle Eye's grandfather and his family escaped from this enemy during a cold winter, but were lost without the food necessary to survive, so the grandfather decided to hunt an animal to relieve his hunger.

After trying to find a kill, he realized he had lost his way back. The great White Buffalo appeared tired and hopeless, showing him the way to his family. The chief said that Eagle Eye would be one of his shamans or a great chief tomorrow.

Russell Means

Oglala-ihanktonwan, a Sioux born in 1940 Russell Means is one of many militant Native Americans who came to prominence in the 1960s.

He provoked controversy by demonstrating that Indians are still an important part of American society at the turn of this century. The childhood experience of being transferred from a reservation school to California, where his Indianness was thrown in his face, partially shaped his career.

Until he met Dermis Banks, who co-founded the American Indian Movement in 1968, he became involved in drugs and crime. Means became a prominent figure in the national media and led numerous Movement demonstrations, most notably the occupation of Wounded Knee in 1973.

In addition, he has served as a defense attorney and has run for vice president of the United States.

He has acted in several films, including The Last of the Mohicans (1992) and Disney's Pocahontas (1995), playing the character Powhatan.

Means remains a leading advocate for Indian causes, even though he is no longer affiliated with the Movement.

Sitting Bull

Sitting Bull (1831-1890), more than any other Indian of the plains, represents the Indian virtues of generosity, courage, tenacity and resistance to white incursions. Demonstrating his generosity at the age of ten, he killed a breed of bison and distributed the meat to the needy. At the age of fourteen he gave his first blow to the enemy and demonstrated his courage. They recognized him as wichasa wakan or sacred man and accepted him in the Strong Heart Warrior Society.

In 1863, he opposed the white to enter the hunkpapa hunting zones, and in 1867, he was appointed chief of the Latvian Sioux nation. Defeating the white soldiers, Sitting Bull had a vision during the sun dance in 1876. A few weeks later, he helped the forces of Lakotas and Cheyenes defeat the soldiers of Custer on the banks of the Little Bighorn River.

Before retiring to a reserve, he took his family to Canada, returned and spent a touring season with Buffalo Bill's Wild West. In 1890, the tribal police arrested him for participating in the dance of the spirits.

Literature

The oral tradition of Native Americans includes a variety of themes, from simple stories with moraleja to the most eloquent sentences. The development of written language and contact with other cultures have enabled indigenous peoples to further expand their forms of expression. Murder narrative, which is common in many native cultures, has served as a basis for the development of written creativity and the emergence of native literature in recent times. This native literature has not only kept traditions alive, but has also served as a bridge between native culture and the predominant white society.

The autobiography, of which there is a long tradition, is probably the most direct means of communicating to a stranger the realities of Indian life. The son of the woods, by William Apess, a northeastern small-sized mestizo, was almost the first book in which an Indian author translated the native experience for non-natives. Apess wrote his autobiography in 1829, in which he spoke of the abuses he and other Indians had suffered from the hands of the whites, as well as his personal religious beliefs. Prominent authors include Luther Bear Erguido, Charles Eastman (dakota santee), John Rogers (ojibwa), and Paula Gunn Alien. (Laguna Pueblo). Some biographies have also had a great impact, such as Black Alce speaks (1923), written by John Neihardt, which tells the life of the visionary Lakota Black Alse.

Both this and similar works, however, lack a genuinely Indian meaning. Not being an Indian, the author has imposed a narrative structure that is not owned by the subject, which causes the narrative to lose authenticity.

Wynema (1891), written by Sophie Alice Callahan, was the first novel by an Indian author. The Dance of the Spirits and the Wounded Knee massacre were important tribal themes in his time. Native writers, some of whom have achieved great success, including kiowa N. Scott Momaday, whose novel House Made of Dawn won the Pulitzer Prize in 1968, have seen the novel as a fruitful genre. Louise Erdrich (ojibwa; see below), Gerald Vizenor (ojisay), Wendy Rose (hopi-mi-wok) and Maurice Kenny (mohawk) were other authors who received awards. The theme of Indian identity and its relationship with the dominant white culture is one of the most common themes in native novel.

Poets such as Gerald Vizenor and Creek Joy Harjo strive to capture the emotional intensity and rhythms of native-speaking language, as native poetry has a more direct connection to oral tradition. This contemporary poetry, like most of Indian literature, is written in English, but strives to maintain the modisms, spirit and content of native American languages.

The written word is important, but it has not replaced the oral tradition, which continues to exist in both English and native languages and serves as much to express ancient wisdom as the current circumstances. The common purpose of written and spoken language is to explain and record the experience of Native Americans, which is often distorted by whites or dismissed as insignificant.

Nativist Movements

Many spiritual movements arose with the intention of helping Indians get used to the arrival of the whites. Anthropologists call these movements "nativist" because they are an effort by indigenous peoples to ensure the survival of their Aboriginal culture in any possible way, as opposed to attempts to assimilate them. Where altered conditions had deprived the old ceremonies of meaning or made them incongruous, as was the case with celebrations in honor of places where the people no longer lived, Native American movements sought to reaffirm the values of the natives.

Nativist movements were divided into two categories: those of "revitalization" and the "millennialists". Both were syncretic, but to varying degrees. In the early movements, the Indians managed to calm white criticism by adopting some Christian formalisms and symbols and eliminating traditional elements that the missionaries considered pagan, satanic or superstitious. Some revitalization movements, such as Lake Beautiful and Native American Church, were organized in congregations similar to those of Christian churches. These movements allowed the core of traditional beliefs to survive disguised as Christianity.

"Millennialists" are another type of nativist movements that tend to be more violent. These movements occurred when the white invasion was so rapid that traditional culture was in danger of collapse. The prophets were in charge of some millennial movements, but not all. Almost all began with a prophet who announced the imminent end of the current system and the return to conventional life.

According to some scholars, contact with the Christian prophetic tradition contributed to the appearance of Indian nativist prophets. The motivation behind the millennial movements can be found in Jesus' call to the Jews to recover their traditional values, as well as in his promise that God would eliminate the current system to establish a spiritual kingdom that would last a millennium (hence his name). However, other experts argue that the native prophets had a background in the Dancing of the Prophet, a common ceremony that included prophecies, exhortations, and trance, which took place before the contact. In any case, the native prophets were innovators eager to share new beliefs and practices with their peoples.

Generally, the prophets appeared in difficult situations, such as those that the Seneca had to endure before the appearance of Lake Beautiful. Many of them were sacred men, such as the prophet paiute Wodziwob, but others lacked spiritual formation despite their oratory or political skills. Almost all became prophets after having had personal dreams or visions.

Beautiful Lake, also known as Large House Religion, was the first major revitalization movement that emerged in the northeast. The syncretic movement began among the Senecas, a town of the Iroquois League, in 1799. The Seneca lands were confiscated, sold or stolen after the War of Independence (1775-1783), in which the Seneca allied themselves with the British. Food was scarce and alcohol consumption increased the risk of social collapse. At that time, Lake Beautiful, the brother of a leader, had a dream about a meeting with spiritual beings, who advised the Senecas to stop drinking alcohol and all dances, except for a "Dance of Adoration".

They were also advised to maintain a peaceful relationship with white citizens. Only the Indians had a heaven and hell in their view of Beautiful Lake. Every week, those who had faith in his Good News gathered in a long house to practice worship. The religion was a great success among the Six Nations and is still practiced. Other movements came to light at the beginning of the 19th century, such as that of the prophet Shawni and the one of the ojibwa prophetess, an unnamed charismatic woman who apparently travelled the northern region of the Columbia River. She may have been the inspiration for the prophet wanpum Smohalla, also known as "The Preacher", who is one of the most famous prophets on the northwest coast. The sacred man Smohalla lived in the valley of the Columbia River and in 1860 he began to preach a message that he believed came from the realm of spirits. His prophecy was based on the fact that if the Indians refused to adopt the practices of the white who would "harm" Mother Earth, such as mining and arading the fields, their fate would improve. Many Dances of the Spirits of the coast and the plains of the northwest were inspired by the prophecies of Smohalla.

Furthermore, Smohalla gave rise to a series of nativist movements in California, where severe cultural degradation gave birth to a rapid succession of movements at the end of the 19th century. The Bole-Maru mixed traditional values with dualistic concepts inspired by Christian religion, such as heaven and hell, God and the Devil. In some villages in California, the Bole-Maru movement is still in operation. The Indian Church of the shakers, founded around 1880, is also similar. Agitators ensure that they receive energy directly from God during trances that are characterized by intense thunderings. Through songs that combine Indian melodies and a mixture of traditional and Christian verses, this Church attaches great importance to the healings of faith. Towards Easter and in August take place its main ceremonies, which include rituals of renewal of the traditional world.

TERRITORIAL CONFLICTS

Current territorial conflicts

Native Americans handed over 810 million hectares of land to the white in 370 treaties between 1784 and 1871. They were almost always signed under coercion or deliberate deception. The Indian territory of the United States was further reduced due to the Dawes General Distribution Act of 1887 and the amendments added until the early twentieth century. By 1934, the area had decreased from 56 million hectares to 14 million. Almost half of this territory was under federal control.

The Indians demanded justice in the courts, and their demands flooded the judicial system. The Indian Claims Commission (ICC) was created by the U.S. Congress in 1946 to meet the demands of Native Americans. None of the cases examined envisaged the restitution of the land requested, but only a financial compensation for the land that had been expropriated.

The ICC remained operational until 1978, when it was dissolved, leaving 68 cases unresolved.

The Western Shoshon claim, whose ancestors signed the Treaty of Ruby Valley in 1863, is one of the most persistent claims. One third of the ancestral land they claim belongs to the state of Nevada, where numerous and important government facilities are located. According to the shoshons, they did not give up their lands in the Ruby Valley Treaty; instead, they allowed the whites to use them. The ICC investigated the case and found that the agreement had been used as an excuse for the illegal expropriation of 10 million hectares of Shoshon land. Despite the fact that the ICC offered a compensation of about 42 cents per hectare, the land price in 1863, the western shoshons have not accepted money in exchange for their land because many of them believe that Mother Earth cannot be bought or sold. Currently, the shoshons have applied to Congress for their territorial claim.

The problems facing Canada are similar. The James Bay case is one of the most tragic, difficult and prolonged in Canadian legal history, as they face the energy company Hydro-Québec, who seeks to build on their lands the largest hydroelectric complex in North America. Hydro-Québec has flooded 11,400 square kilometres of land and caused ecological damage on another 17,600 square miles. The fish is said to be affected by mercury contamination caused by the decomposition of trees and plants, and it has been found that in the bodies of some elderly people there is a level of Mercury 20 times higher than the acceptable level. The government has advised farmers to stop eating fish in response. During the George River Caribbean migration in 1984, more than 10,000 animals were killed by a sudden discharge of water from the Caniapiscau basin. Continuing environmental problems have reinforced the Crisis' opposition to the project and their demands for conscientious environmental studies before building new dams. The Cris and other Canadian indigenous communities have urged the government to intervene, but the government's response has left them confused and frustrated.

In addition, Indian nations face territorial disputes due to cultural differences, the reserve system and the challenges of population growth. Often, these conflicts are complicated by intervention by government or energy companies eager to know with whom to negotiate the use of disputed land. In one of these conflicts, the hopis confront the southwestern navajs (dineh). The Arizona hopis share their traditional territory with the Navajo.

The Navajo Reserve completely surrounds the Hopi Reserve. Both tribes worship the earth as sacred and claim to be descendants of it. The agreement of 1882 established the hopi reserve with the promise to "protect" the other Indian inhabitants of the area. In the shared reserve of 1882 there were about 1,800 hopis and 400 navajo, however, the Navajo population increased significantly compared to the hopi. In 1900, the hopis were about 2,000 while the Navajo were already 7,500, while today there are about 10,000 Hopis and 275,000 Navajo. In 1950, there were more hopis than hopi in the reserve, and by 1968, tribal tensions between these known enemies began to exacerbate. The hopi reserve was officially divided in 1974 when Congress intervened to separate the two villages.

More than 364,000 hectares of hopi land and an additional 162,000 ha were granted to the Navajo as compensation for the 5,000 Navajo who were forced to abandon the new and diminished hopi reserve. Only one hundred of the hopis had to abandon the lands reserved for the Navajo, despite the loss of half of their reserve. However, the conflict has not come to an end due to the long years of dispute, the opposition of the Great Mountain Navajo to move and the constant attention of the press. This case has set a precedent for tribes seeking to receive land instead of money, instead, from their lost territory. But there are still many problems to solve, the most important of which is that the hopis have not received land or money in exchange for the land that was lost. In addition, social costs have increased due to the problems caused by the resettlement of shipyards.

The way in which Canada resolved one of these conflicts demonstrates positive progress in the process of recognizing the territorial rights of indigenous peoples. The Nunavut Territorial Claim Agreement, which the Inuit ratified in 1992, was approved by the Canadian Parliament in June 1993. In this way, the definition of a new autonomous territory called Nunavut ("Our land" in inuktituk, the Inuit language) was established, which will begin to have legal validity at the beginning of the twenty-first century. The ancestral land of the Inuit is Nunavut, where they have lived for thousands of years in the eastern and central Arctic. Under the agreement, they will receive 350,000 square kilometres and more than one billion Canadian dollars payable over 14 years, in addition to the right to hunt and harvest, as well as equitable representation in nature, resources and environmental management agencies. They will share with the federal government the rights to explore gas, oil and minerals in the Crown lands; they will retain minerals rights on ten per cent of the land, as well as the right to negotiate with industries established in Inuit territory. Three additional national parks will be established.

Crow Creek

The burial of Crow Creek has established a model for relations between Indians and archaeologists on the subject of ancient tombs. In 1978, archaeologists at the University of South Dakota found the bones of 500 people who died in a slaughter that occurred during a war between the ancestors of the arikaras around 1325 at the Crow Creek Reserve. The Sioux and the Arikara were traditional enemies, but they worked together to protect the remains. At first, they asked not to touch the bones, but when the robbers began to damage the place, it was agreed that they would move to study them, provided they were returned to them. The bones were buried again near where they were found in 1981.

Wounded Knee

The Wounded Knee Massacre, a dark episode of American history, took place on December 29, 1890 in the Pine Ridge Indian Reserve, located in South Dakota. This tragic event marked a chapter of brutality in relations between Native Americans and the United States government.

The conflict began when a detachment of the 7th Cavalry Regiment, led by Major Samuel Whitside, intercepted a group of Lakots from Chief Si Tanka near Porcupine Butte Peak. The soldiers escorted the Lakots to the Wounded Knee stream, where they encamped. Later, the rest of the 7th Cavalry Regiment, commanded by Colonel James W. Forsyth, arrived, surrounding the indigenous camp and carrying four Hotchkiss cannons, which predicted an imminent tragedy.

On the cold morning of December 29, American soldiers entered the camp to disarm the Lakots. The situation became tense when a member of the tribe named Yellow Bird refused to hand over his rifle, claiming that it had cost him a lot of money. The forcex became violent and, in the middle of chaos, the rifle fired. The detonation was like the spark that lit the powder.

The 7th Cavalry Regiment opened fire indiscriminately against the Lakotas, killing men, women and children, even some American soldiers were wounded or killed in the shooting. The Lakota warriors who still had weapons responded to the fire, but were quickly shot down by the numerical and arms superiority of the American forces.

The result was devastating. At least 150 members of the Lakot tribe lost their lives, including unarmed women and children. Some estimates raise the number of indigenous people killed to more than 300, mostly women and children. In addition, 25 soldiers of the 7th Cavalry Regiment were killed and 39 others were wounded in the confrontation.

Surprisingly, the 20 regiment members who caused the most casualties among the indigenous peoples were awarded the prestigious Medal of Honor, a recognition that has been the subject of controversy and condemnation in subsequent years.

In 2001, the National Congress of American Indians issued resolutions condemning the award of these medals and requesting the United States government to withdraw them. Despite the tragedy and controversy, the site of the massacre has become a National Historic Landmark, a shady reminder of a tragic episode of American history that must not be forgotten.

In the pre-conflict years, the U.S. government continued its policy of looting land from the Lakot tribes, while the unrestrained hunting of bison in the Great Plains, their main source of food, left them on the verge of extinction. The treaty promises to protect the land from reserves from invasion by settlers and gold-seekers were not fulfilled as agreed, causing riots in reserves.

During that time, the news of a Paiute prophet named Wovoka spread among the reservation tribes. Wovoka founded the Dance of Spirits religion and preached that the Christian Messiah, Jesus Christ, had returned in the form of an American Native. According to his vision, the white invaders would disappear from the native lands, the ancestors would lead the natives to thriving hunting lands, bison and other animals would return in abundance, and the spirits of the forefathers would return to Earth. All this would be achieved through the solemn Dance of the Spirits, performed by dragging the feet in silence at the rhythm of a single drum.

However, the Dance of Spirits movement was not only a religious expression, but also a response to the cultural devastation suffered by the native tribes. Their lands were usurped, their herds of bison disappeared, and their way of life collapsed. They increasingly depended on the U.S. government to survive.

American settlers were concerned to see the tribes of the Great Plains and the Great Basin participate in the Dance of the Spirits, fearing that it might trigger an armed conflict. American Indian agent James McLaughlin decided to arrest Lakota leaders to stifle what they called the "Messiah's madness." Buffalo Bill became a key intermediary, but the situation became violent when they tried to arrest Toro Sentado.

On December 15, 1890, a violent clash resulted in Toro Sentado's death, which led to his Hunkpapa band fleeing to the Pine Ridge Reserve to join the Spotted Elk leader. Tensions grew, and the authorities sought solutions.

This turbulent era represents a crucial moment in the history of relations between Native Americans and the United States government, marked by the despair of native tribes and the struggle to preserve their ways of life and beliefs.

The great mound of the serpent

A large zigzag landscape rolls and slips over a prominent summit surrounded by steep wooded slopes and steep cliffs in Adams County, Ohio. The Grand Serpent Mount is a low and rounded terraplen of just

over 380 meters long, 6 meters wide and 1,20 meters high. It is like a snake that stretches as it challenges, with seven rings stretched out and three rings wrapped in the tail.

Although we do not know who built this monumental building, it is possible that it was created by the culture of Adena, which flourished in the area between 500 BC and 200 AD. Although no dateable objects have been discovered in the snake itself, 122 meters away there is a conical-shaped sepulchre mound that is related to the culture of Adena. A characteristic of both Adena's and later Hopewell's culture was the construction of mounds.

In 1886, the terraplen suffered severe damage due to the activity of treasure-seekers and curious, in addition to the deterioration caused by soil erosion. When P. W. Putnam of Harvard University's Peabody Museum rescued and restored the site, the monument seemed destined to become a maize.

The Grand Serpent Hill became a state park in 1900 and a viewpoint was built for visitors. Currently, the monument, despite its official character, is threatened by urbanists who want to rebuild the Brush stream and build an artificial lake and a spa near the site, as well as by oil and mining companies that could destroy the mound for gas, oil and uranium.

The terraplen is so extensive that it can only be seen in its entirety from the air. The large amount of land that was moved, possibly in baskets, to build the efigie proved that the builders were very efficient and well organized. Per hundreds of people took many years to finish the work.

It is perceived that the figure holds a large oval object between its jawbones. The mound is believed to be a snake that eats an egg. In many Aboriginal cultures of the United States, ofidiums play an important role, which has generated a variety of theories about the meaning of mounds. Because of the lack of solid evidence, any assumption about the precise function and purpose of the Great Snake Mount is purely speculative.

It is possible that the mound was created by the Adena culture, whose name comes from another Ohio site. The cultures of Adena and Hopewell, which later appeared in the Illinois and Ohio regions, built large tombs for large-sized people.

The Bear's Hill (Bear Butte)

From the Bear Butte hill, which rises 1.350 metres above the plains of South Dakota, you can see to the west the imposing peaks of the Paha Sapa (Black Mountains), while to the east extend large meadows that reach the horizon. Many peoples in the plains regard it as a sacred place, including the Lakotas Sioux who call it Mato Paha (or "Bear Mountain") and the Cheyenes who refer to it as Noavasse (or the "Magic Refuge"). Many lakotas and cheyenes come to the hill every year to pray and fast.

The hill is in conflict with that want to build a tourist and recreational area. It is part of Bear Butte State Park, which is administered by South Dakota. During the most important Indian ceremonies, visitors are forbidden access to the summit. Nor can they use the areas of fasting and searching for visions, nor the ceremonial trails. But many Indians complain that the authorities have contaminated the hill by building parking and camping areas at their feet, as well as a tourist climbing piste on the hillside itself. Despite the prohibitions, some areas considered sacred have also been invaded.

With regard to the 1978 Indian Religious Freedom Act, the Lakotas and Cheyen spiritual leaders filed a complaint before a federal court against the state. The court found that the interests of Indians were more relevant than the State's obligation to guarantee public access to a site of geological and historical importance and to protect visitors.

The verdict was confirmed by the Court of Appeals in 1983, but the Supreme Court refused to consider the case. Despite this, the Lakotas and Cheyenes continue to protect these sacred sites.

The Lakotas believe that the Bear Hill was formed as a result of a fight between a giant bear and a monster named Unkchegila. The hill indicates the location where the bear suffered fatal injuries. The top of the hill, which is the highest point in a radius of many kilometers, is an ideal place for the Hanbleceya or the solitary search for visions for the Lakotas. This was where Crazy Horse, the famous Lakota chief, had a vision of a bear with supernatural abilities in 1876. Shortly thereafter, Crazy Horse led the Indian forces that defeated Custer's troops at Little Bighorn.

According to Cheyen tradition, the mythological hero Mutsoyef (Sweet Medicine) gathered a council on the hill, to which wise men from all communities of the planet attended. Mutsoyef received from Maiyun, the Great Spirit, four sacred arrows that gave him great power over the bison and people.

The train.

Americans of European descent saw railways as a great innovation. What the white men called progress was nothing more than a blow to the traditional lifestyle of the Aborigines, as has happened so many times.

Although many Indian tribes opposed the arrival of the railroad, in 1891 there were four rail lines connecting the United States with Canada and a fifth, the Canadian Pacific, crossing Canada.

The influence of the railway was devastating for the Plain Indians - whose livelihoods were based on bison meat, skin, bones and tendons - because bison hunting from trains became an entertainment for travellers.

Between 1869 and 1890, when the Union and Central Pacific railways merged, train hunters reduced the number of bison from six million to just a thousand.

Schools for Indians

Although western-style schools were established in most Indian reserves with the aim of accelerating assimilation, internments for Indians in the United States and Canada were also established. Children were expelled from their homes and often spent most of the year in nursing homes, where they remained until adulthood.

The goal was to "kill the Indian... and save man," according to the founder of the Carlisle Indian School in Pennsylvania. Students were forced to learn English, convert to Christianity, take Western classes, and reject their own clothes, languages, and religious beliefs. Although a small group adopted the white culture, the majority lost their confused cultural identity.

Indigenous students

Indigenous peoples were traditionally educated by listening to and observing their elders, and then collaborating with them in the tasks of daily life. Indian children sat at the feet of the narrators, whose accounts of warriors, peacocks, and other spiritual beings gave lessons of morality, philosophy, and religion. Afterwards, they began to assume responsibilities as adults, such as collecting and preparing food and medicinal plants, tracking tracks, hunting, and manufacturing clothing and tools.

Schools abandoned this traditional form of teaching. Both reserve schools and boarding schools, which separated children from their families for ten months a year, attempted to assimilate the Indian and Inuit peoples, disconnecting the kids from their traditional culture. Although the education policy of Indians is somewhat less rigorous today, most indigenous young people still attend public schools. Although education in these schools has little to do with the more flexible and individualized tribal method, the main problem lies in the fact that the state school system reflects the traditions and values of the dominant white society, which often contradict traditional teachings. As a result, many Indians leave school without the necessary preparation to develop properly both in their own culture and in that of the society that dominates them.

Some organizations such as the American Indian Movement have sought to establish model schools for Indians in recent years in order to offer education more sensitive to Indian traditions. The first survival school for indigenous peoples was established by the Minneapolis Movement in 1971 with the aim of helping young Indians adapt to white society without losing contact with their own culture. After that, native-run elementary and secondary schools were established. These native schools take into account traditional festivities and activities. For example, at the Nunamiut School in Anaktuvuk, Alaska, October classes are focused on the harvesting of strawberries, a traditional Inuit activity.

Native schools also have problems in higher education. There were no native universities until 1968. That year, he founded and led the first native university in the Arizona Navajo Reserve. Other tribal groups hurried to do the same. The American Indian Consortium for Higher Education (AIHEC) was founded in October 1972 by six tribal community universities. Currently, AIHEC has 30 members in the US and Canada. The AIHEC has become a very useful tool to help the economic development of Indians and to maintain the continuity of their cultural traditions. More than 20,000 Indian students are currently attending tribal universities, located in or near the reserves, and their programmes range from technical or vocational subjects to postgraduate courses. But his interest in Indian culture is the most important. At the Sioux Rosebud Reserve in South Dakota, there is a training in "Cultural Resource Management" that teaches indigenous youth to collect and administer oral tradition, as well as to find and preserve historical and archaeological heritage.

Until the seventh generation

In the tradition of many Indian nations, seven is a very important number. The Lakotas mention seven "original persons" and possessed Seven Council fires. Seneca culture distinguishes between "seven talents".

The pawnees relied on the position of the Seven Stars (known by Europeans as the Pleiades) to determine the beginning of the ceremonial year. First, several Native Americans assume responsibility for those who follow their example, even up to the Seventh Generation.

This means you have to think about what you do in the future. Some Indians look forward to the future byining traditions in new and non-traditional ways, such as novel writing or the practice of other arts. Some struggle to regain what they believe is the "balance of the world", demanding the restitution of the remains of their ancestors and other ancient relics found in museums, and demanding that land that was illegally expropriated be restored.

Some attempt to provide employment to the unemployed or preserve their culture by educating young people in their own traditions, although they also give them the means to compete in the modern world.

Languages

The study of native languages, many of which were not written until recently, has been based mainly on reports, generally not systematic, from anthropologists, linguists, missionaries and other people who came into contact with Indian peoples. As diseases and other calamities devoured entire nations, several languages and dialects were extinct. Many natives abandoned their mother tongue due to assimilation pressure. Indian children were punished for speaking their own language in hospitals run by religious and state organizations. However, a large number of native languages are still spoken: Navajo is the language spoken by approximately 100,000 people. In other situations, only a small group of elders can use the common language, as in the case of the osage, which is only spoken by half a dozen individuals.

The linguistic diversity is notable in a relatively small population such as India (a little over a million and a half inhabitants). It is estimated that about 300 Indian languages may exist, which in turn can be divided into about 2,000 dialects. At least 57 language families include atapasca, iroquesa, muskogi, salish, and sioux. In California alone, there are twenty different language families, representing a greater diversity than that found throughout Europe. Seventeen more linguistic families can be found west of the Rocky Mountains, while the remaining twenty are found in the rest of the North American continent. According to the researchers, the 57 families are organized into six "macrofamilies" or groups: esquimal-aleutian, na-Dené, macro-algonquina, macrosio, aztec-tanoana and hokan. Some experts go further and suggest a single macrofilum, the "amerindian", which is the ancestor of all native languages. Although they have attempted to connect Indian with Asian languages, most experts believe that Indian is too theoretical.

The great diversity of languages was due in part to the geographical isolation of many peoples, which caused great disparities in dialects of the same root, as happened among the tsimshian, whose various dialects are incomprehensible to those who speak one of them. It is important to consider the possibility of multiple migrations from Asia at different times. But the constant movement of people across the continent was the most important cause. The languages of the peoples that have come as far away as the dogribs (from the Northwest Territories) and the Navajo and Apache (of the southwest of the U.S.), all speak Atapasco languages, can relate to each other.

In addition, there was a great deal of pollution between some languages and others. Each tribe adopted words from other tribes and from the white population.

Some words, such as tipi sioux, were integrated into the vocabulary of Indians and whites. Original terms, such as "powwow" and "caucus", were incorporated into American English. Many names of provinces, states, cities and geographical places in the United States and Canada have their Indian origins, such as Connecticut (which means "Long River"), Ontario (who means "Spainful Water") and Chicago (what means "Onion Field"). The development of free and hybrid languages for commercial and other purposes was due to linguistic contamination. The sign language of the prairie Indians was the most well-known lingua franca. On the northwest coast, traffickers used the "chinook jargon", a combination of European words and chinook.

English has completely overtaken many native languages today as a lingua franca. However, many languages are coming back to life, including some that were thought to be extinct, such as the gros-ventre, which was no longer spoken when ancient recordings were found in a museum; now, young gros-ventrers are learning their ancestral language. Many Indian schools teach the tribal language, and universities also include native language classes. For example, five Indian languages are taught at the University of Oklahoma.

The Battle of Little Bighorn

Until recently, the world had only known the white image of cough in the last four centuries of American history. The Battle of Little Bighorn, also known as the last confrontation of Custer, is an example. This is an attractive legend. A group of American cavalry were ambushed on the Little Bighorn River, Montana, on June 25, 1876. Indian warriors from the plains surrounded the soldiers. The soldiers, despite their large number, fought with great courage until only one man remained: General George Armstrong Custer. On the top of a hill, surrounded by the bodies of his soldiers and horses, this hero of the war of secession, whose blonde hair reached to his shoulders, resisted and fired until he fell to the ground. As a result, the battle became the most famous event of the Indian wars and the humiliating defeat became an example of the indomitable spirit of the pioneers. Military, officials, artists, and historians contributed to this version. According to legend, no one survived to mention the story of the last confrontation and the white Americans accepted the official version.

The Sioux, Arabah and Cheyen warriors, as well as their families, were many who survived that battle. The U.S. military was always subjective, but their testimony was ignored because they were Indians and therefore inclined. A coherent picture of the battle can be found in the accounts of the oral tradition of the Indians, which coincide with the archaeological finds. The clash at Little Bighorn was a disorderly riot that lasted just over half an hour instead of a last heroic and prolonged clash.

The Battle of Little Bighorn was a monumental confrontation that left a deep mark on American history. The scene was a vast Montana field, where the combined forces of the Lakots, Cheyenes and Arapajos, led by the temerary Crazy Horse, confronted the 7th Knightry Regiment of the United States Army, under the command of the bold Colonel George Armstrong Custer.

The army of Crazy Horse was an impressive and varied force, composed of seven tribes (hunkpapas, sans arc, black feet, miniconjou, brule, cheyenes and oglala), as well as women, children and a vast herd of cargo and livestock for subsistence. While estimates vary, it is believed that the full contingent could have ranged between 6,000 and 9,000 individuals, with around 3,000 warriors and an astonishing sequence of 30,000 animals.

At the heart of this powerful army, the spiritual leaders of the Sioux played a vital role. Sitting Bull led the hunkpapa lakota, Red Horse to the minneconjous, Two Lunas to the cheyenes, Crazy Horse at the sioux oglala, Gall to the lakota siounan and Rain in the Face to the Northern cheyennes.

However, the battle became a disaster for Custer and his men. (escuadrones C, E, F, I y L). There have been speculations about several reasons that could have contributed to the defeat. First, Custer may have underestimated the magnitude of the Indian force and overestimate the ability of his regiment to overcome it. His confidence in the risky cavalry loads that had succeeded in the Civil War could have led him to make hasty decisions.

Another factor contributing to the defeat was the division of Custer's forces on the battlefield, which could have been an attempt to prevent other commanders such as Terry or Gibbon from stealing him the merit of victory. Custer also refused to equip himself with heavy weapons, such as the Gatling machine guns, and did not seek support forces because of his desire to enter combat immediately.

In addition, he disobeyed the advice of his native explorers, who advised him to expect reinforcements, as they were at a numerical disadvantage over the Indians. The rush to attack and win before July 4th, American Independence Day, and the Democratic Party Convention, where Custer had political aspirations, also influenced his hasty decisions.

These strategic and judgmental errors led to an overwhelming defeat for Custer and his regiment, with the tragic loss of 268 men, including 16 officers, as well as 10 civilians and explorers. In comparison, indigenous casualties were much smaller, with about 50 warriors and 10 civilians.

However, a more modern theory suggests that a wound in Custer's chest, inflicted while trying to cross a fence and attack the village, could have contributed to the collapse of his regiment. This theory also raises the possibility that the subsequent war council, which blamed Custer, was used to cover up the responsibility of other commanders such as Reno and Benteen.

The Battle of Little Bighorn, with its complex circumstances and its impact on history, continues to be the subject of debate and study by historians and enthusiasts of military history.

In a painting by Edgar Paxson, Custer and his soldiers, including the painter's brother, courageously but uselessly repel the Indians at Little Bighorn. The battle is depicted in the Sioux drawing as the dispersed chaos in which it actually became.

However, Paxson is true in one aspect: Custer cut his famous hair shortly before the fight.

The Native American Church

The Native American Church, sometimes called the peyote cult, is one of the most important revitalization movements. It is a pan-Indian movement that has 250,000 followers.

Its origins go back to Mexico and after the decline of the Dance of the Spirits, it began to spread throughout the fields. In their ceremonies, members of this Church consume peyote, a hallucinogenic cactus, to have visions.

From sunset to dawn, meetings take place in a tipi under the direction of a boss or driver who moves from one group to another, and they use carracks, bone scissors and other traditional utensils. The doctrine of the Church combines Christian and Christian traditions. Jesus and

God are protective spirits. They follow some of the Ten Commandments and believe in the ideal of fraternal love. They don't drink alcohol. Peyote was forbidden for some time, although it was only used as a sacrament. Currently, the Native American Church permits its use, but many whites insist it is illegal.

The Impact of Christianity

The French Jesuits were strange individuals with black socks carrying gifts and the promise of eternal life, which led the Hurons to mistrust them. Despite having lived in the villages of the Hurons and having learned their language, the Jesuits were not willing to live the same life as these Aborigines, rejected Indian spirituality and pressured the people to accept the teachings of a foreign religion.

The sacred figures of the Christian narrative inhabited an unimaginable and distant land instead of a territory that the tribe knew and could enter, despite the fact that the Christian God was a great spirit compatible with the beliefs of some Indians. Christian teachings were based on a book that the Indians could not read and were expressed through images, symbols and music that were foreign to them.

In any case, the missionaries managed to convert the converts. For many, Christianity was a question of economic opportunism. The furons discovered that wearing French clothes allowed them access to the leather trade. In 1610, Chief Micmac Membertu and other members of his family were baptized by the French Recolet missionaries in Port Royal, in present-day New Scotland, for the possibility of establishing an alliance with the French.

The settlers who caused these suffering were the same ones who offered Christianity as a solution to the suffering of the natives. For the Timucua of Florida, conversion was a way of reducing the exploitation of the Spanish conquerors. Similarly, the northeastern Mohawks asked for missionaries after the French destroyed their villages in a punitive incursion in 1666.

Converts were forced to reject traditional beliefs and rituals, which were the very essence of their culture and identity. To secure submission, the Puritan settlers of New England used force. In 1662, the wampanoag, who were practically slaves, were persecuted for hunting and fishing during the day of keeping, using Indian medicines, and marrying outside the Catholic Church. The Indians of Plymouth, Massachusetts, were sentenced to death for denying Christianity. The 19th-century Anglican Lego minister William Duncan urged the tsimshian of the northwest coast to destroy their own masks, clothes and other religious symbols. These acts were common. The Federal Office of Indian Affairs issued a code of religious offences in 1883 prohibiting natives' medical practices and sun dancing, among other rituals. The Canadian government banned potlatch at about the same time.

Roman Catholicism had a great influence because many of its traits had resonances known to the converts: the worship of the virgin evoked the respect they felt for Mother Earth, saints resembled Indian sacred beings, and spectacular ceremonies were a feature shared by Catholics and many Indian cultures.

Although Christianity spread among some indigenous groups, in many peoples it did not supersede traditional religion. Respect for the natural world, a fundamental feature of many native American traditions, was barely mentioned in this religion. Christianity was a foreign doctrine to most Indians because they were brought to India by people whose influence was not considered positive.

Modern Medicine

Traditional healing methods were severely affected by the European conquest, among other things because many natives were affected with new diseases that decreased the population of their communities. Western medical methods were introduced by traffickers, missionaries, and military doctors, and since the early 19th century, the US government has hired doctors to visit Indian children in reserves and hospitalized during epidemics. More than 20 treaties were signed around 1870 to ensure medical care to specific tribes. The Indian Health Service (IHS), which provides basic medical care to most reservations, emerged from those agreements. However, Indians still do not have the same medical services as the non-Indian population.

Loss of land

In the post-United States century, there were warriors in each tribe willing to fight the American army, which generally faced overwhelming obstacles. Black Hawk, a Sauk leader who led the resistance in the Mississippi Valley in 1832; Manuelito, a Navajo leader who was active from 1863 to 1866; Lone Wolf, a Kiowa leader in the Red River War (1874-1875), which took place in the Southern Plains; and Dull Rnife, a Cheyenne leader who fought in the Central Plains and led an impressive captivity escape in Fort Robinson, Nebraska, in 1879.

The revolts led by these leaders failed, forcing the survivors to endure humiliation and pain due to their failure. Some chiefs, such as the Crazy Horse of the Sioux, continued to resist and eventually died in captivity. Others, such as Jerome, experienced a decrease in their spirit or, like the Sitting Bull and Chief Joseph, spent the rest of their lives in captivity, generally far away from their homes. Until the end, they cared for the well-being of their people, which, in the case of the Sitting Bull, cost him his life.

The leaders of the resistance keep their spirit in today's native leaders, who are more calm but also determined. The right to live in an Aboriginal American society continues to be defended by activists such as Dermis Banks and Russell Means, as well as by administrators and politicians such as Wilma R Mankiller, an academic activist and former head of the Cherokee nation, or Nellie Cornoyea, the inuvialuk who was appointed head of government of the Canadian Northwest Territories in 1991. These leading figures seek compensation for historic losses of land and indigenous peoples, as well as securing educational and economic opportunities that contemporary American society often considers false.

Native leaders also have more power because they have political control in the same assemblies and legislatures that voted for the withdrawal, confinement and destruction of their people. In 1990, Elijah Harper, a member of the Manitoba legislature, made a decision not to approve the Meech Lake Accord, a draft that sought to modify the Canadian federal constitution to meet the demands of French-speaking Quebecers, who wanted to be considered an independent society in Canada. Harper rejected a bill that did not guarantee the same rights for the Aboriginal people of the nation.

In recent times, the reputation of spiritual leaders such as Black Eagle has grown due to the prevailing cultural trends in the predominant white society. Those who continue to maintain native traditions have also introduced Aboriginal American art to the world. Most prominent artists include Charles Edenshaw and Bill Reid, who carve in the traditional Haida style, the hopi jeweler Charles Loloma, the washo basket weaver Datsolalee, and the Inuit sculptors and printers Etungat and Kenojuak. In addition, there are many writers, actors, dancers and playwrights whose creation, sometimes with Western touches, has helped highlight the beauty, dramatism and intensity of North American Aboriginal culture.

The opposite side of the story

The first European explorers, guided by Indian guides, traveled rivers and lakes in the same boats, shared food and experienced the same environmental difficulties.

When the natives first saw the Europeans, they were surprisingly surprised. In an ancient micmac story about the arrival of the white man, it is said that the first European ships saw floating islands on the horizon, with some trees being cut down, and some even thought they had seen bears climbing through the branches. The early European merchants fascinated the natives with already known objects, although made from wonderful and novel materials: knives that were not of stone but of sharp steel, copper furnaces that did not break in contact with fire and glass counts in a wide range of magnificent colors. Obviously, they felt that the weapons were magical. The noisy, heavy, annoying firearms that the early white men carried with them were more useful for the tactics of secrecy and surprise of the Indian warriors than the silent arrows and the bow for quick launches. While a firearm magically ended an enemy or animal from afar in an open and closed eye, the bow was only effective on short distances.

The great European discovery journeys were hardly ever driven by the desire to explore new lands and cultures. The main reason for the adventurers was the opportunity to expand Europe's markets and resources. When Spanish, French, English and Russian explorers, merchants and settlers met with North American indigenous peoples, they did not think of the possibility of reaching an agreement with them. They did not see the rich cultural diversity when they arrived with the attitude of conquerors, but a people who seemed to lead a rudimentary life in the midst of poverty. Moreover, they saw it as an opportunity to exploit the land and its many resources.

The idea that European material civilization represented the culmination of world achievements influenced the perception of the natives as economically poor people, despite having lived well on their lands for countless generations. Other peoples were lagging behind, because they lived on the margins of divine punishment or because they were considered inferior beings. Until well into the eighteenth century, both the Spanish and the English Puritans had an attitude towards the North American Aborigines based on this perspective. Christian doctrine believed that nature should be subordinated to humanity, controlled and conquered rather than imitated or treated on an equal footing; therefore, Europeans were not impressed by the way in which the natural world was an inseparable part of the culture and spirituality of the Indians. In the 19th century, Charles Darwin's evolutionary theory reinforced European beliefs that Indians were considered "low". Thus, they were regarded as degraded beings who survived a once great race or a slowly evolving people.

Thus, there was no shared language and a shared worldview at the base of relations between the Aborigines and the Whites, and the feeling that everyone was human barely developed, at least on the part of the Europeans. As more settlers moved to the "New World", the lack of understanding between them resulted in a tragedy for the Native Americans. The Indians owned some resource-rich areas, but did not believe that the land was a personal possession. Indians, be they hunters or gatherers, learned to share to survive and make the most of their effectiveness, following the rhythm of seasons and moving from place to place to meet their needs. As a result, the exchange of land for commercial goods and, subsequently, for money must have generated in them a great sense of unreality. Per they rejoiced that Europeans were willing to pay for the right to take advantage of lands they considered free.

The optimism, based on a lack of knowledge of European legal norms, soon turned against the Aborigines with whom territorial negotiations were carried out. In addition to staying, the white refused to share the land from the moment they signed an agreement or treaty. As for the whites, if the Indians could not prove that they possessed the land legally, they were forced to surrender it by force or by agreement.

Reserves

The creation of reserves in the era of white expansion was initially intended to keep Indians completely separated from white society. Later it was believed that the marginalization of the native culture would accelerate the incorporation of Indians into the dominant society.

The idea of establishing exclusive areas for indigenous peoples originated in the "cities of prayer" in the 17th century. In the decades immediately following American independence, the first reserves were established in the northeast in the modern sense. As the demand for land by the whites increased, the authorities renounced the appearance ofining tribal integrity, despite the fact that they used to be part of the homeland of each group. In a few decades, native peoples of farmers and foresters settled in unknown territories, overturning thousands of years of cultural adaptation to specific environments.

In 1825, the United States government proposed a definitive solution to the "Indian question": establishing a large Indian country west of Mississippi. The proposal, which was officially known as Indian territory in 1834, included the present-day Kansas, Oklahoma and parts of Nebraska, Colorado, and Wyoming. The five south-eastern villages that were displaced received the first reserves. Over a period of time, they achieved a higher level of economic prosperity and literacy than some nearby states. In any case, the changes caused by the war of secession in the sixties of the 19th century led to the economic crisis. At the end of the war, the tribes had to sign new agreements and ced land to the Comanches, Kiowas, and Cheyen, as well as to remote communities in the north. More than 65 different tribes and bands lived in the future Oklahoma, along with farmers, hunters, friends, enemies and strangers.

Even before the Civil War, white colonization occupied Indian territory. The Indian lands considered "inviolable" were gradually converted into states, and in 1907, when Oklahoma obtained this status, the Indian territory disappeared. The 29 tribes of Oklahoma controlled only 26,000 hectares in 1975.

To accelerate the assimilation of the Indians, tribal lands were allocated to individual owners, which increased the loss of territory. The Dawes General Distribution Act of 1887 aimed to divide tribal land into plots of no more than 64 hectares, a policy that departed from Indian decentralization customs. The result was the loss of 38 million acres of reserve land. The last attempt to dismantle these lands was in 1953, when the U.S. Congress decided to re-buy the land from the reserves. Prior to the failure of this policy, 19 tribes lost more than one million hectares of land.

Over the past decades, this trend has been fostered through the resolution of certain territorial conflicts. Historically, Canada has followed a similar process of confining Indians in reserves, although with less severity than in the United States. According to the pact established in the early 1990s, the Northwest Territories should be divided between the West Indians (Denes and Métis) and the East Inuit.

Forced displacement

At first, the departure of Native Americans from their lands was a discreet process. The missions from New France (northeast of Canada) to Florida confused the Indians, who did not notice the abuses of the colonists by handcuffing cloths, cooking sticks, weapons, knives and other useful and ready-to-use items. Coastal areas and river valleys soon became forbidden territories for indigenous peoples because the early colonizers were attracted to fertile, well-irrigated lands close to waterways.

Many small southern coastal tribes fled into the interior because of the demand for Indian slaves in the English colonies of America and the sugar plantations of the Antilles. The Indian groups attacked each other because they had to compete for decreasing territories and resources. They often joined the colonizers because they were seduced by payment in commercial goods. In 1704, James Moore, who was the British governor of Carolina, arrived in Florida, which was under Spanish control, along with a group of settlers and a thousand creek, apalachic and yuchis natives. The Apalaches, the Timucua and the Calusas, who had already been subdued by the Spanish occupation, were virtually eliminated and returned with more than 6,000 captives destined for the slave market. To the north, Indian tribes also faced conflicts due to pressure from European colonization and competition for the thriving leather trade. The Iroquois League, led by the Dutch and the English, dispersed the Hurons and forced the Ojibwas to settle in the Western Great Lakes, where the Sioux were forced to intern in the plains.

As the United States won the War of Independence (1775-1783), the Iroquois lost their homeland and fled to British Canada. When the Crown bought all the land in Canada without respecting the rights of the Aborigines, Indian territories also disappeared.

In 1787, the United States Congress passed the Northwest Ordinance, which stated that "Indians will never have to lose their land and property without their consent". However, the constant presence of the Indians was considered an obstacle to white colonization, and those beautiful words were soon empty of meaning. From time to time, small groups of natives were expelled or exterminated by gangs from North and South Carolina to California. Initially, the official measure was to remove them from areas intended for white settlers and to place them in small areas of unfavourable land. In 1830, President Andrew Jackson took a further path when he enacted the Aboriginal Expulsion Act, which forced Aborigines to move west of Mississippi and give the east to the whites. Although in theory the Indians had the ability to reside in their own "Indian territory", in reality the expansion of the White to the west was carried out without interference.

The displacement trauma was controlled through intense military activities. For example, New Mexico volunteers attacked its territory in the 1950s under the leadership of Colonel Kit Carson. After the last battle at the sacred site of Chelly Canyon in 1864, the Navajo surrendered. To reach Fort Summer, New Mexico, more than 8,000 people, mostly on foot, had to travel 480 kilometers of mountain and desert. Many people died on the way. After several decades of intense suffering, the survivors were allowed to return to a reserve located within their original territories.

Encrypted speakers

During the wars of the twentieth century, Indian citizens collaborated in almost every division of the United States armed forces, despite their long-standing animosity towards the military. The Aborigines saw these services as a way to preserve their ancient warrior customs and, in general, contributed voluntarily.

The ability to speak in languages that the opponent did not know is one of the advantages obtained. During World War I, the Germans who had joined the Allied lines could not understand what the encrypted speakers said. Cochtaw. The U.S. Army Signal Corps used troops from various Indian nations during World War II. Most importantly, the Marine Corps had 420 navals to send the most important messages among the Allied forces in the Pacific.

The Japanese failed to decipher the messages. Recruited Navajoes invented new words to describe unknown military ideas. The submarine was nicknamed "iron fish", for example.

Live past

Many Indians believe that their ancestors and other ancient beings are among themselves and are not far from the living. Each individual joins his ancestors in other states of being, including the present, when he dies. A European speaker could say: "My grandfather lived in the twentieth century and Sitting Bull in the nineteenth century", while an Indian speaker might say: 'My grandpa and Setting Bull are here'.

Many indigenous groups remember the living presence of their ancestors in stories and works of art. For example, the peoples of the northwest coast lived in a pictorial universe full of visual representations of Cuervo, Orea, and other sacred ancestral beings, most of whom were responsible for the great events that created the world and its inhabitants.

They were always present in images carved into totems, houses, canoes, clothes, dancing suits, masks, ceremonial containers and various everyday household utensils.

Historical Claims

Upon taking possession of Indian lands, white scientists were enthusiastic about investigating the life and origin of the Indians, hoping that they would soon disappear. The U.S. Army was ordered to obtain skulls from indigenous people for study at the Army Medical Museum in 1867. Thousands of skulls were collected in battlefields and cemeteries. During subsequent decades, several major museums and universities gathered collections of skeletons and funeral objects for their study and exhibition. Some private collectors plundered tombs and then sold or exhibited human remains and funeral objects as tourist attractions.

These acts are sacred to Native Americans. Many traditionalist Indians believe that the deceased still exist, albeit in a different world, and that the transfer of their remains constitutes an affront to the dignity of the ancestors and a threat to the delicate harmony of nature. For decades, indigenous peoples struggled to recover and bury these remains. Finally, in 1990, Congress passed the Native American Tomb Protection and Repatriation Act, which obliges all official agencies to return human remains, funeral objects and sacred objects to the peoples from which they were taken, as well as to consult the tribes directly before excavating in Indian sites.

The campaign to recover the lands that the Indians lost in wars and treaties has not been so successful. The legal battle began in 1946 when the U.S. Congress established the Indian Claims Commission, which established compensation for illegally seized land, equivalent to the value of the land when it was usurped and more interest. This helped peoples whose claims were met to generate significant incomes. For example, the Passamaquoddy of Maine received sufficient funds to implement educational, industrial development and housing programmes. On the contrary, some communities refused to accept money, arguing that the land is sacred and cannot be bought or sold. Canada recognizes that Indians have rights based on traditional occupation, unlike the United States. The government's goal is to reach agreements that include land delivery and economic compensation. The creation of the Inuit territory of Nu-navut has been the most notable consequence of this policy. However, there are still many cases that have not been resolved.

In November 1969, shortly after the government closed down the Alcatraz prison in San Francisco, about 200 indigenous people took control of the island and requested its restitution to the Indian people. His claim was based on a clause in a treaty that promised to return to the Indians the territories that were no longer useful to the federal government. The operation continued until 1971, when the last occupants were expelled by the federal police. Subsequently, however, other demonstrations occurred, such as in 1972 a march called "The Road to Broken Treaties" in Washington D.C., which was controlled by the Office of Indian Affairs for six days.

The return of Ahayuda

Many Indian peoples in recent times have demanded that museums return their sacred objects to ensure the survival of traditions. The New Mexico Zuñis celebrated the success of their campaign to recover the wooden images of Ahayuda, the twin gods of war, which had been transferred to the Smithsonian Institution around 1880. On the winter solstice, every two years, sacred men place the images in the shrines that dominate the Zunji people and perform a ritual to ask for the protection of the gods.

In 1978, the Zuni requested the restitution of the efigies. Despite long talks with the Smithsonian Institution, the museum eventually ceded due to the growing demand for Indian sacred objects across the country. The Zuñis have received more photos of Ahayuda from other museums.These acts are sacred to Native Americans. Many traditionalist Indians believe that the deceased still exist, albeit in a different world, and that the transfer of their remains constitutes an affront to the dignity of the ancestors and a threat to the delicate harmony of nature. For decades, indigenous peoples struggled to recover and bury these remains. Finally, in 1990, Congress passed the Native American Tomb Protection and Repatriation Act, which obliges all official agencies to return human remains, funeral objects and sacred objects to the peoples from which they were taken, as well as to consult the tribes directly before excavating in Indian sites.

The campaign to recover the lands that the Indians lost in wars and treaties has not been so successful. The legal battle began in 1946 when the U.S. Congress established the Indian Claims Commission, which established compensation for illegally seized land, equivalent to the value of the land when it was usurped and more interest. This helped peoples whose claims were met to generate significant incomes.

For example, the Passamaquoddy of Maine received sufficient funds to implement educational, industrial development and housing programmes.

HAU DE NO SAU NEE "PEOPLE WHO BUILD"

Message to the Western World

Hau de no sau nee is the name of the Confederation of Six Nations or Iroquois that groups the Mohawks, Oneidas, Onondagas, Cayugas, Senecas and Tuscaroras. These villages were located in the northwest of North America. Their culture and relationship has been studied with great curiosity and dedication, as it enabled horizontal relationships between human beings and prevented a vertical hierarchy from establishing power relationships in the community.

In 1977 they formulated three papers that masterfully synthesized their vision of the cosmos, nature and living beings and, of the history of mankind; these were presented to the United Nations Non-Governmental Organizations. This is the first of them:

Hau de no sau nee, or Confederation of the Six Iroquois Nations, has existed on this earth since the beginning of human memory. Our culture is among the oldest continuously existing cultures in the world. We still remember the earliest events of human beings. We recall the original instructions of the Life Creators in this place that we call Etenoha: Mother Earth. We are the spiritual guardians of this place. We are the Ongwhehonwhe the Genuine People.

At the beginning, we were told that human beings walking on Earth have been provided with all the things necessary for life. We were instructed to carry love from one another, and to show respect for all beings on this Earth. We were shown that our life exists with the tree life, that our well-being depends on the welfare of the Vegetable Life, that we are close relatives of the four-legged beings. In our ways, spiritual consciousness is the highest political form.

Ours is a Lifestyle. We believe that all living beings are spiritual beings. Spirits can be expressed as forms of energy manifested in matter. A grass leaf is a form of energy manifested in matter: grass matter. The spirit of the grass is that invisible force that produces grass species, and it manifests itself to us in the form of real grass.

All things in the world are real, material things. Creation is a real material phenomenon, and Creation manifests itself to us through reality. The spiritual universe, then, manifests itself to Man as Creation, the Creation that sustains life. We believe that man is real, a part of Creation, and that his duty is to sustain life in conjunction with other beings. That's why we call ourselves the Ongwhehonwhe - the Genuine People (o Real).

The original instructions indicate that as we walk on Earth we have to express great respect, affection, and gratitude towards all the spirits that create and sustain Life. We congratulate and thank the many supporters of our lives: the corn, the porot, the calf, the winds, the sun. When people stop respecting and expressing gratitude for these many things, then all life is destroyed, and human life on this planet will come to an end.

Our roots lie deep in the lands where we live. We have a great love for our country, because it is where we were born. The soil is rich with the bones of thousands of those of our generations. Each of us was raised in such lands, and it is our duty to take great care of them, because from these lands the future generations of the Ongwhehonwhe will sprinkle. We walk through them with great respect, because the Earth is a very sacred place.

We are not a people who demand or demand anything from the Creators of Life, but instead, we greet and thank that all the forces of Life are still in action. We deeply understand our relationship with all living beings. To this day, the territories that we still preserve are filled with trees, animals and other gifts of Creation. In such places we still receive our food from our Mother Earth.

We have seen that not all people on Earth show the same kind of respect for this world and its beings. The Indo-European people who have colonized our lands have shown very little respect for the things that create and sustain Life. We believe that such people ceased their respect for the world a long time ago. Many thousands of years ago, all the peoples of the world believed in the same Way of Life, that of harmony with the universe. They all lived in accordance with the Natural Ways.

About ten thousand years ago, people who spoke the Indo-European languages lived in an area today known as the Russian Steppes. At that time, they were a people of the Natural World who lived on the earth. It had developed agriculture, and it is said that it had begun the practice of domesticating animals. It is unknown that it was the first town in the world to practice the domestication of animals. The hunters and gatherers who wandered around the area probably purchased livestock from the farmers, and adopted an economy based on gathering and raising herds of animals.

The assembly and breeding of animals pointed to a fundamental distortion in the relationship of humans with other forms of life. It set in motion one of the true revolutions of human history. Before herds, humans depended on Nature for the reproductive powers of the animal world. With the advent of flocks, humans assumed the functions that through time had been the duties of the spirits of animals. Time after that happened, the story records the early emergence of the social organization known as "patriarchy".

The area between the Tigris and the Euphrates rivers was the home, in ancient times, of several peoples, many of whom spoke Semitic languages. The Semitic peoples were among the first in the world to develop irrigation technology. This development led to the initial emergence of settlements, and eventually cities. Water manipulation, another form of spiritual life, represented another style in which humans developed a technology that reproduced functions of Nature.

Within these cultures, a hierarchically stratified social organization crystallized. Ancient civilizations developed imperialism, partly because of the very nature of cities. Obviously, cities are concentrations of population. More importantly, these are places where the material needs of such a concentration must be imported from the countryside. This means that the Natural World must be subjugated, squeezed and exploited according to the interests of the city. To order this process, the Semitic world developed early codes of law They also developed an idea of monotheism to serve as a spiritual model for their material and political organization.

Much of the history of the ancient world relates to the struggles between the Indo-European and Semitic peoples. Over a period of several millennia, the two cultures impacted and combined. In the 2nd century BC, some Indo-Europeans, more specifically the Greeks, had adopted the practice of building cities, thus engaging in the process they called "Civilization".

Both cultures developed technologies similar to such civilizations. The Semitic peoples invented marmitas that enabled the creation of woodworking for trade and the accumulation of surpluses. Those primitive marmitas became ovens that could generate enough heat to melt metals, notably copper, tin and bronze. The Indo-Europeans developed the way to melt iron.

Rome was the heir to these two cultures, it became the place where the final encounter took place. Rome is also the true birthplace of Christianity. The process that has come to be the culture of the West is historically and linguistically a Semitic/Indo-European culture, but has been commonly defined as Jewish-Christian tradition.

Christianity was an absolutely essential element in the initial development of this kind of technology. Christianity advocated one God. It was a religion that imposed itself exclusively on all others. The local people of the European forests were a people who believed in the spirits of the forests, the waters, the hills and the land; Christianity attacked such beliefs, and effectively despiritalized the European world.

Christian peoples, possessing superior armaments and a need for expansion, were able to militarily subdue the tribal peoples of Europe.

The availability of iron led to the development of tools that could cut down the forest source of charcoal to make more tools. The new lands, cleared of trees, were then worked by the newly developed iron plow that was, for the first time, pulled by horses. With such technology, far fewer people could work much more land, and indeed many men were displaced to become soldiers or landless peasants. The rise of such technology ushered in the Feudal Age and eventually made possible the emergence of new cities and expansive trade. It also marked the beginning of the end of the European forest, although it took a long time to complete the process.

The eventual building of cities and the concomitant emergence of the European State created the onslaught of expansion and search for markets, which led men, such as Columbus, to spread sails across the Atlantic. The development of sailing ships and navigation technologies made the "discovery" of the Americas inevitable.

The Americas provided Europeans with a vast new area for expansion and material exploitation. Initially, the Americas supplied new materials and even finished materials for the developing world economy that was founded on Indo-European technologies. European Civilization has a history of peaks and declines as technologies reach their material and cultural limits. The finite Natural world has always provided a kind of intrinsic contradiction to Western expansion.

The Indo-Europeans attacked every aspect of North America with unparalleled viciousness. The Native peoples were ruthlessly destroyed because they were an element that could not be assimilated by Western civilizations. The forests provided materials for large ships, the land was cool and fertile for agricultural surpluses, and some areas provided sources of slave labor for invading conquerors. At the time of the Industrial Revolution, in the mid-19th century, North America was already a leader in the area of developing extractive technologies.

The hardwood forests of the northwest were cut down to provide agricultural timber. Those forests were destroyed to create charcoal for the forges of iron smelters and blacksmiths. By 1890, the West had turned to coal, a fossil fuel, to supply the energy needed for the many forms of machinery that had been developed. During the first half of the 20th century, oil replaced coal as an energy source.

Western culture has been horribly exploitative and destructive of the Natural World. More than 140 species of birds and animals have been completely destroyed since the European arrival in the Americas, mostly because they were unusable in the eyes of the invaders. Forests were flattened, waters polluted, Native peoples subjected to genocide. The vast herds of herbivores were reduced to mere handfuls, the buffalo was almost extinct. Western technology and the people who have employed it have been the staggeringly most destructive forces in human history. No natural disaster has destroyed on such a scale. Not even the Ice Age had so many victims. But just like hardwood forests, fossil fuels are also finite resources. As the second half of the 20th century progressed, people in the West began to look for other sources of energy to fuel their technology. Their eyes have fallen on atomic energy, a form of energy production whose by-products are the most poisonous substances that man has ever known.

Today the species of Man faces the question of the very survival of the species. The way of life known as Western Civilization is on a deadly path for which its own culture lacks viable answers. When faced with the reality of its own destructiveness, it only manages to advance to more efficient terrains of destruction. The appearance of Plutonium on this planet is the clearest sign that our species is in trouble. It is a sign that many Westerners have chosen to ignore.

The air is rotten, the waters are poisoned, the trees are dying, the animals are disappearing. We think that even the climate systems are being modified, our ancient teachings warned us that if Man interfered with Natural laws such things would happen. When the last Natural Way of Life is gone, all hope of human survival will be gone with it. And our Lifestyle disappears quickly, victim of destructive processes.

Hau de no sau nee's other documents have outlined our analysis of legal and economic oppression.

But our essential message to the world is a basic call to consciousness. The destruction of Native cultures and peoples is the same process that has destroyed and is destroying life on this planet. The technologies and social systems that have destroyed animal and plant life are also destroying Native peoples. That process is Western Civilization. We know that there are many people in the world who can quickly discern the intent of our message. But experience has taught us that very few are willing to search for a method to determine any real change. If there is to be a future for all beings on this planet, we have to begin looking for avenues of change.

The processes of colonialism and imperialism that have affected the Hau de no sau nee are just a microcosm of the processes that affect the world. The reservation system used against our people is a microcosm of the system of exploitation used against the entire world. Since the time of Marco Polo, the West has been refining a process that has mystified the peoples of the Earth.

The majority of the world does not find its roots in the culture of Western traditions. Most of the world has its roots in the Natural World, and it is the Natural World, and the traditions of the Natural World, that must prevail if we are to develop truly free and equitable societies.

It is necessary, at this time, that we begin a dynamic of critical analysis of the historical processes of the West, to expose the real nature of the roots of the exploitative and oppressive conditions that force humanity. At the same time, as we gain understanding of these processes, we must reinterpret that history for the people of the world. Ultimately, the most oppressed and exploited people are the people of the West. They carry the weight of centuries of racism, sexism and ignorance that have made their people desensitized to the true nature of their lives.

We have to consciously and continually challenge every model, every program, and every process that the West tries to impose on us. In his book Pedagogy of the Oppressed, Paulo Freire wrote that imitating the oppressor is a characteristic of the oppressed, to obtain relief from the oppressive condition through such action. We must learn to resist such a response to oppression.

The people who live on this planet need to break the narrow concept of human liberation, and begin to see liberation as something that needs to be expanded to the integrity of the Natural World. What is needed is the liberation of all the things that sustain Life - the air, the waters, the trees - all the things that sustain the sacred fabric of Life.

We feel that the Native peoples of the Western Hemisphere can continue to contribute to the potential survival of the human species. Most of our people still live according to traditions that have their roots in Mother Earth. But Native peoples need a forum where our voice can be heard. And we need alliances with other peoples of the world to assist us in our struggle to recover and maintain our ancestral lands, and to protect the Way of Life we follow.

We know that it is a very difficult task. Many nation-states may be threatened by the position represented by the protection and liberation of peoples and cultures, of the Natural World, a transformative orientation that must be integrated into the political strategies of the people that seek to defend the dignity of Man. But such a position continues to grow in strength, and represents a necessary strategy in the evolution of transformative thinking.

Native, traditional peoples hold the key to reversing the processes that in Western Civilization promise an unimaginable future of suffering and destruction. Spiritualism is the highest form of political consciousness. And we, the Native peoples of the Western Hemisphere, are among the surviving bearers of such a type of consciousness in the world. We are here to impart that message.